PRAISE FOR
THE INSIDE INNOVATOR

"Louis Gump was one of the first people to talk to me about expanding access to information by giving people news on their mobile devices. While it is commonplace now, at the time it was transformative. He brings those same types of insights in his new book, *The Inside Innovator*. He also demystifies the term 'intrapreneurship' and makes the process accessible to people who wish to excel as leaders within larger companies. Whether you are a neuroscientist like me or in a totally different discipline, this book can help you harness your natural talents."

—SANJAY GUPTA, Associate Chief of Neurosurgery, Chief Medical Correspondent, #1 *New York Times* and *Wall Street Journal* best-selling author

"Drawing from my own global experience in nurturing intrapreneurial talent, Louis's book is a powerful tool for any leader seeking to drive innovation, growth, and success within their organization."

—RALPH DE LA VEGA, former Vice Chairman, AT&T

"As a former colleague, I watched Louis lean into mobile products long before anyone could imagine the products or benefits. *The Inside Innovator* offers unique insights to empower you to create meaningful change *within* a company!"

—WONYA LUCAS, former President and
CEO, Hallmark Media

"*The Inside Innovator* is full of excellent, practical advice on how to be a more effective intrapreneur, regardless of the stage of your career. Even with forty-five years in the intrapreneuring field, I still learned new ways to move ideas forward and manage setbacks. Louis Gump writes in a style that is clear, succinct, and graceful, which makes his years of experience in both intrapreneurship and entrepreneurship shine brightly to deliver lessons that are profoundly practical."

—GIFFORD PINCHOT III, coiner of the word "intrapreneur,"
author of *Intrapreneuring: Why You Don't Have to Leave the
Corporation to Become an Entrepreneur*

"The time is right for this book. The faster things change, and the more disruptions we encounter, the more urgent it is to constantly adapt, rethink, reimagine, and rewire. Intrapreneurs are the people who make that happen. They're always asking, 'Is there a better way?' Organizations need to ask themselves, 'How good are we at creating intrapreneurs?' Those that promote a culture of learning rather than knowing, encourage ownership at all levels, and develop leaders with the skills to nurture these inside innovators are the ones that will shape the future. Thank you, Louis Gump, for showing us a workable path forward."

—QUINT STUDER, author of *Rewiring Excellence: Hardwired to Rewired*

"In *The Inside Innovator*, Louis Gump uses his experience as an intrapreneur to create an incredibly relevant and insightful guide. Having worked closely with Louis and witnessed his remarkable skills in navigating the corporate landscape, I can attest to his profound understanding of intrapreneurship. His strategic thinking, coupled with his innovative spirit, has consistently driven growth and success in several large organizations. This book encapsulates his valuable wisdom and serves as an essential resource for anyone wishing to spark innovation within a corporate setting."

—LISA CHANG, Senior Vice President and Chief People Officer, The Coca-Cola Company

"Sometimes we look at the newest leadership books with a jaundiced eye as we reluctantly consider someone's new take on the same tired, old ideas. Louis Gump's outstanding new book is different. *The Inside Innovator* is a well-written, insightful, and engaging guidebook on the leading-edge concept of intrapreneurship that will inform you, challenge you, and open the aperture of your thinking as you take in the valuable ideas and best practices he offers in this excellent work. This is a book you will carefully read, want to share with friends, and refer to repeatedly in the years ahead. I highly recommend it!"

—RANDY HAIN, President of Serviam Partners, executive coach, author of *Essential Wisdom for Leaders of Every Generation* and *Upon Reflection: Helpful Insights and Timeless Lessons for the Busy Professional*

"Building new growth initiatives inside a global media company presents a whole host of challenges, which requires skillful navigation, future focus, business acumen, integrity, and a generous dose of optimism and zeal. Louis infused a sense of possibility mixed with practicality while he led the transformation of CNN's mobile business during the evolution of our digital platforms. Louis is an unusually self-aware leader, knowledgeable and comfortable in sharing his values, with the ability to rally a multiplicity of stakeholders around the mission. In *The Inside Innovator,* he draws on his experiences to provide a uniquely valuable perspective on how to really get innovation done."

—SUSAN GRANT, Executive Vice President, CNN News Services (retired)

"Louis Gump has put his finger on, perhaps, the only hope organizations have to thrive in the future. Thanks to rapid change, cultivating innovators within established organizations will no longer be a luxury but a necessity, and this book shows you how to do just that. Employers beware: More than seven in ten teens plan to be an entrepreneur after graduation. If you hope to hire and retain them, you'd better create a place for them within your team."

—TIM ELMORE, Founder and CEO, Growing Leaders, author of more than 30 leadership books, including *A New Kind of Diversity*

"It's amazing that this book has not been written until now. *The Inside Innovator* is a comprehensive guide to creating new lines of business within an existing company. Drawing from his own experiences and a wide network, Gump works through the many factors that determine whether a new venture is successful. He is especially insightful in discussing when and how an intrapreneur needs to act differently than an entrepreneur in a corporate context. This is not something you read about in the business press, and thoughtful readers can learn a lot from the lessons he and his collaborators have learned through their wide-ranging experiences. Companies need successful intrapreneurs to evolve and grow—and often these opportunities are the most fulfilling and rewarding part of a career. Finally, we have a book that focuses on this essential process!"

—JOE FIVEASH, VP Strategy and Media Solutions, Watson Media and Weather, IBM

"Louis thoughtfully and uniquely elevates the concept of intrapreneurship to its rightful place alongside entrepreneurship as a driving force of innovation and growth in our economy. His work will bring inspiration and confidence—as well as a comprehensive playbook—to those working to keep established enterprises at the forefront of their industries."

—CANNON CARR, CEO, CornerCap Wealth Advisors

"Through Louis Gump's insightful and actionable book, I am reminded of my early days pushing for innovation in seemingly rigid structures. His strategic approach to intrapreneurship provides not just validation but also an arsenal of tools for those ready to take on the challenge."

—ANNE SCHELLE, Managing Director, Pearl TV

"Intrapreneurship demands resilience, innovation, and a balance of risk-taking and strategic alignment. As intrapreneurs, we navigate corporate landscapes to ignite change, blending entrepreneurial spirit with the resources and scale of larger entities to forge impactful innovations. In *The Inside Innovator*, Louis Gump has given us a guidebook to do this in a way that creates lasting change within established organizations, while creating a magnifying effect within industries and the people who benefit from the innovation."

—GREG STUART, CEO, MMA Global

THE INSIDE INNOVATOR

A PRACTICAL GUIDE TO INTRAPRENEURSHIP

LOUIS K. GUMP

FAST COMPANY
Press

Fast Company Press
New York, New York
www.fastcompanypress.com

Distributed by Greenleaf Book Group

For ordering information or special discounts for bulk purchases, please contact Greenleaf Book Group at PO Box 91869, Austin, TX 78709, 512.891.6100.

Design and composition by Greenleaf Book Group
Cover design by Greenleaf Book Group
Cover Image: Golden-egg-with-shell;
used under license from Shutterstock.com

Publisher's Cataloging-in-Publication data is available.

Print ISBN: 978-1-63908-094-6

eBook ISBN: 978-1-63908-095-3

To offset the number of trees consumed in the printing of our books, Greenleaf donates a portion of the proceeds from each printing to the Arbor Day Foundation. Greenleaf Book Group has replaced over 50,000 trees since 2007.

Printed in the United States of America on acid-free paper

24 25 26 27 28 29 30 31   10 9 8 7 6 5 4 3 2 1

First Edition

This book is dedicated to the intrapreneurs, past, present, and future.

You create extraordinary value and change the world, while engendering professional growth and personal fulfillment.

CONTENTS

INTRODUCTION

In the late 1990s and early 2000s, entrepreneurs were all the rage.

They graced the covers of business magazines. Their exploits filled the news cycles. Investors showered them with money and so many well-deserved accolades. It seemed as if the world's success and energy had established a new center of gravity in Silicon Valley.

Meanwhile, I worked for a large media company in Atlanta. As a member of very talented teams, I'd already built a career helping customers grow using technology-based services. Immediately after serving in smaller firms, I was pleased to have started this new role at a bigger company. I knew the size of the organization and its brand strength could present lots of opportunities. Our team members clearly saw the changes around us—in our company and in the broader business landscape. In that first decade of the new millennium, it was becoming increasingly clear that if media moguls didn't participate more fully in this innovation explosion, we would all be run over by the Entrepreneur Express.

Even with numerous opportunities to innovate across the country and around the world, Silicon Valley's center of gravity sometimes still seemed far removed from my daily work. From my perspective, entrepreneurs were often solo flyers—independent and talented individuals working on their own or with relatively small companies. I, on the other hand, was engaged in corporate teamwork. I had labored for years to develop the skills of engaging with groups of smart, talented, and committed people in the service of a larger corporate mission. The entrepreneurial mandate had spread through the business world, and we all heard some form of this: create new businesses and innovate! But for those of us in the corporate world, that mandate was more complicated to carry out. Innovation often seemed like a very individual process. What could a mission-driven team in a rowboat on the corporate ocean do?

The answer is: plenty. And that's what this book is about.

Far too often, business leaders assume that innovation is best suited to the entrepreneurial world. Innovation demands agility. It demands risk. It demands an ability to color outside the lines and think outside the proverbial box. Big companies often have difficulty doing that. But they can. And they do all the time.

Often, intrapreneurs just don't get the same attention as entrepreneurs do. This book will shine a light on the efforts that go on behind the walls of some of the most successful and forward-looking companies. This is the work of the in-house innovators, the corporate explorers—the intrapreneurs.

What is an intrapreneur?

An intrapreneur creates value through innovation and growth, inside a larger organization. In many cases, the intrapreneur builds a new growth business within this broader environment. While the exciting new upstarts may grab many of the headlines, intrapreneurs near and far are creating new products, services, and businesses that shape industries. They do this in companies ranging from global business titans to local market leaders, from charitable nonprofits to government entities, from educational institutions to informal community groups and beyond. What's more, intrapreneurs often innovate at a scale few startups can match, while working closely with entrepreneurs.

Entrepreneurs, of course, are also innovators. They lead and grow their own independent businesses. They are doing important work and deserve recognition for their risks and accomplishments. But they are more likely to do their work in the spotlight. Investors and news media watch them. Intrapreneurs, by contrast, work mostly behind the scenes. You can find them in their companies, at industry events, and sometimes helping entrepreneurs achieve breakthrough moments in their smaller partner companies. But generally, not on the cover of *Fast Company* or in the lead article of Axios. As a result, the best practices of intrapreneurs often go unnoticed and unrecorded.

The two roles differ in important ways, and understanding the uniqueness of each is critical to success.

Intrapreneurship is not just entrepreneurship for the salaried set. It is its own practice, with its own set of critical skills. In this book, I pull back the curtain further on the practice of intrapreneurship and show what it takes to drive innovation from the inside. This is not a criticism of entrepreneurs—far from it. Instead, it's an exploration of the ways in which those inside companies also contribute to the innovation community. When you understand how an intrapreneur differs from an entrepreneur, you can dramatically increase your ability to drive innovation within an organization.

In more than two decades of in-house innovating and close collaboration with large companies, I've seen what works and what doesn't from multiple vantage points. I've been the intrapreneur in a big firm. I've been the entrepreneur in a small firm. While serving as CEO of two small companies, I've worked closely with talented intrapreneurs at big ones to create new opportunities. And conversely, while serving as an intrapreneur, I've worked closely with leaders of small businesses as they achieved more of their own potential, too. We accomplished a lot together thanks to the active involvement of highly talented and dedicated teams. In these pages, I share what it takes to be a successful intrapreneur.

Over the years, I've seen approaches that achieved spectacular results and some that didn't work as well. I've known many people who have had similar experiences as they reshaped industries. I'm very grateful for a range of educational opportunities and work experiences early on that provided me with a valuable foundation for intrapreneurial work. At the same time, I also ended up learning a bunch of things related to intrapreneurship the hard way. I want to make it easier for you. This book is designed to provide insights and shortcuts to success and to increase your success rate sooner as you work hard to make a difference in the world.

In this book, you find what I wish I'd known all those years ago at the dawn of the dotcom era. This book lays out how corporate teams can become groundbreaking intrapreneurial game changers.

While this type of unheralded innovation has long served as a source of value creation, it first got its modern name in 1978. Husband and wife team Gifford Pinchot III and Elizabeth Pinchot published a paper titled "Intra-Corporate Entrepreneurship" while attending the Tarrytown School for Entrepreneurs in New York. The first formal academic case study of intrapreneurship was published in June 1982 on the intrapreneurial creation of PR1ME Leasing within PR1ME Computer, Inc.

In 1985, Gifford Pinchot III expanded his published work with a book titled *Intrapreneuring*. In it, he defined the term "intrapreneur" as follows: "Any of the 'dreamers who do.' Those who take hands-on responsibility for creating innovation of any kind within an organization. The intrapreneur may be the creator or inventor but is always the dreamer who figures out how to turn an idea into a profitable reality."[1] I agree with Pinchot on the substance of this definition. I also would add that an intrapreneur is a corporate explorer, a person who is willing to go to new places and try new ideas and see new things in the process of creating the value referred to in this definition.

Recognition of intrapreneurs continued to gain momentum. Also in 1985, *TIME* magazine published an article titled "Here Come the Intrapreneurs." Later that year, *Newsweek* published an interview with Apple Chairman Steve Jobs in which he described the internal Apple Macintosh team as intrapreneurial. They were, he said, a group of people in a big company going back to the behavior and mindset of startups to produce innovations.

By 1992, the term had made its way into *The American Heritage Dictionary*—as well as many a performance review and job description. The demand for innovative, creative behavior in a large corporate setting was on the rise.

Since then, intrapreneurship has been more explicitly recognized in corporate circles around the world. But even with that track record, the process is often poorly understood. Despite considerable commentary on the topic directly and indirectly, there is still no widely recognized authoritative source on it. Instead, intrapreneurs must re-create the process for themselves over and over again. The concept of intrapreneurship is well known, but its practical implementation remains mysterious for far too many people.

We address this problem in these pages, with guidance and practical information I wish someone had imparted to me when I was wondering how our corporate team could ever be as innovative as an entrepreneur. This is the practical, hands-on guide for those who want to excel at intrapreneurship. In addition to describing my own experiences, I've interviewed a range of accomplished organizational innovators to gather their views and wisdom as well. They shared with me their experiences as intrapreneurs, what they've learned from and about the process, and how they see the practice evolving in today's marketplace. I've listened closely to them and layered in their insights to expand the relevance and utility of this book.

From the start, I wanted to include insights and stories from a range of accomplished people who have been there and done that, who can really add value for intrapreneurs. Little did I know how inspiring that approach would prove to be.

The people I have spoken with have turned out to be some of the very leaders who work quietly and in impactful ways to make lives better for others, many on products and services that millions of people use daily. We're not talking about mythic figures here, and we're not talking about people who live on a pedestal 24/7. They're real people who are doing and have done real work resulting in successes and failures, using their strengths and weaknesses. They are leaders and innovators and tinkerers who have navigated demanding paths while securing deep and broad success with others.

As much as I already expected them to lend valuable insight, the result was even better than I had dared to imagine—a true treasure trove that elevated the learning journey for me, too. I thank them here and hope you will also benefit from their comments now included in this book. The people I reference typically are well-known in their organizations, and yet often less visible outside their own communities. I want to shine a light on them, a sample cross-section of true local heroes, achievers, and innovators just doing their thing, making music in their spaces.

Beyond that, I've worked with literally thousands of intrapreneurs over the years and have learned so much from so many. The quotes and examples included in this work are intended to be a representative sample to illustrate points, not a comprehensive overview of all those I know who are doing impactful work. While I wish that space and time would allow even more people to be recognized, I'm excited about the opportunity to highlight some of the most impressive individuals I know here.

Lastly, I want to acknowledge the vast number of intrapreneurs and their team members beyond those I have interviewed, personally worked with, and know about for one reason or another. So many individuals are doing great work where they are, around their city, their region, their country, and beyond.

To this end, I encourage you to find other people who excel in their own fields as you extend your own learning and career journey. Please consider this a starting place, a foundation, and a reference guide.

This distilled work, built from personal experiences and countless interactions, is designed to help you achieve more professional success, strengthen relationships while lifting others up, increase personal fulfillment, and ultimately contribute to our communities along the way.

The book is organized into two sections:

- In Part I, we focus on the early steps for an intrapreneur. We look at both the internal and external work that should be done to lay the foundation for successful intrapreneurship. This section addresses the intellectual and emotional elements of the intrapreneur and outlines ways to implement familiar business practices early on to establish a strong start. It covers the foundational elements an intrapreneur must usually establish in order to achieve the highest success.

- In Part II, we move into the business activation phase of the combined innovation and growth experience. The content in this section includes the best ways to build a team, communicate, and activate the new intrapreneurial effort. It also demonstrates why an intrapreneurial project does not stop at the company walls. Many of the most successful intrapreneurs must engage in their communities, growing beyond the scope of their employers and connecting with networks and associations in the wider industry.

I want to note here that these phases are not necessarily sequential, nor are they always discrete. They are modular. The actual practice of intrapreneurship typically involves multiple types of activity at the same time. This is one of the reasons intrapreneurship is both art and science, method and intuition, perception and discretion. As with the process of building for most major achievements, it's helpful to understand the component parts in order to blend them together into a unique combination that best suits your circumstances.

Very few people are successful in business simply by good luck. Most attain success for themselves, their companies, and their industries by crafting and honing critical skills. This is true whether you are a young Silicon Valley upstart with VC backing, one of thousands employed by a Fortune 500 stalwart, or any of the companies and other organizations in between and beyond. The business world needs new and creative ideas from many directions. No one can sit out the innovation era. No matter how big your company may be, you have the ability to serve as a driving force for the Next Big Thing.

Innovation happens in-house all the time.

Here's how to do it right.

PART I

LAY THE FOUNDATION

In this section, we explore the critical first steps of intrapreneurship.

First, innovators should look inward, considering the skills, mindset, and principles that resonate for them. To evaluate fit, they should then compare resulting self-knowledge to the needs of successful and fulfilled intrapreneurs. This process will align the individual with an environment that creates the most value while feeding strong relationships and yielding personal fulfillment.

Next, we walk through ways to identify and evaluate promising growth opportunities. While many options typically present themselves to a thoughtful intrapreneur, only a smaller subset will deserve the full attention of the team.

Building on these steps, we then advance to developing a plan to show others why your idea deserves support from the broader organization. Even if you see the opportunity clearly, you will need the active involvement of others to realize its potential.

Address these topics early to ensure success.

CHAPTER 1

START WITH
YOUR INNER GAME

How ready are you for intrapreneurship?

You might be wondering what I mean by *ready*. Clearly, if you're reading this book, you're interested in the topic. But does that mean you're *ready*? Whether you're an active intrapreneurial team member, intend to jump in as an intrapreneur in the future, or simply want to understand the practice better, you must be more than just interested to excel at intrapreneurship. You must engage with focus and commitment.

Yet, knowing if you're ready isn't always a quick process. For the aspiring or practicing intrapreneur, a highly valuable step in being ready is taking an inner inventory of who you are and what you need. Many successful inside innovators begin by looking inside themselves. This may be an in-depth exercise or just a top-level gut check or both. Regardless, this examination ensures that your intentions align with your talents and needs.

You also have to know yourself and your abilities. I'm not talking as much about specific skills. Quite a few of these will be required for basic proficiency in a given role and others can be learned. That said, I'm shining more of a spotlight on a place that often gets little attention in the business process: your inner world. By making the connection between your own capabilities and the demands of the intrapreneurial process, you will better assess how you can be most effective and fulfilled.

Define Your Terms

Part of looking within is to make sure you're the right fit for intrapreneurship. An initial step in understanding this is to be clear on terms that you use for the fit assessment process—both in your thinking and discussions with others. In particular, the definitions of intrapreneur and entrepreneur are similar in their ultimate goals to create value through innovation. But they have different methods of achieving these goals.

Intrapreneurship means serving as and acting like the owner of a business or major growth project within a larger organization. It means that you create value as part of this effort. It often involves innovation in its various forms, including products, services, processes, technology, and others. You take personal responsibility and accountability for growth, even if the broader company has lots of resources (more about this later). In many ways, this role does mean acting like an entrepreneur within a larger organization. However, the skill set, practices, and growth paths for the intrapreneur differ in important ways from those of an entrepreneur in a standalone business.

Intrapreneurship is essential to the health of businesses over time. Debora Wilson, legendary leader at The Weather Channel who led the team that built the original weather.com website before going on to become president of the company, observes the following:

> I think it's really important for organizations whose products are maturing to have intrapreneurial focus because it's one of only two ways to keep a business with maturing products vibrant. This is because every company's product lines, including their related revenue and profit sources, mature over time. So, if you're not starting new sources of revenue and profits, or new products or services, or whatever it might be internally, you have to acquire them.
>
> And acquisitions are risky. They're done all the time. But a lot of times, they don't work out because of a few reasons, and one is that you may not be getting what you thought you were going to get. Maybe there's just a misalignment from a culture standpoint between the organizations. Or maybe you overpay and so there's disappointment. While there are risks involved with internally creating new sources of revenue and profit, I actually think the risks are lower than acquisition risks. I think that's a key reason to focus on it.
>
> But then a really, really important one is that there's a unique set of capabilities and experiences and skill sets that are either created or further developed, amongst your

employee set because, presumably, if you have intrapreneurial activity occurring, at least some portion of your base organization becomes part of that group. And those people are forever changed in a good way because of that experience, so you have a more vibrant and expanded skill set within your organization, which can only be good.[1]

INTRAPRENEURSHIP IS DISTINCT FROM OTHER DISCIPLINES

Intrapreneurship has a specific combination of characteristics that make it unique.

Some have referred to intrapreneurship as corporate entrepreneurship. I want to acknowledge the thoughtfulness and impact involved in using this description. And it is true, these two areas have many similarities. However, there are risks in using this term.

Intrapreneurship is not just a derivative form of entrepreneurship. And without context, this term can give the impression that intrapreneurship is simply the same thing in a different place. My experience is that intrapreneurship has its own characteristics and related behaviors for success. Try being an entrepreneur with all the same behaviors inside most large companies and you will create results ranging from major unnecessary friction to avoidable failure.

Also, intrapreneurship is closely identified with innovation. Most successful intrapreneurs actively advance innovation in their organizations. But intrapreneurship is not just corporate innovation. Corporate innovation can take many forms from industry-changing lines of business to modest process improvements to obscure experimentation in skunk works labs. Intrapreneurs, on the other hand, are focused on the types of practical innovation and growth that create true value for customers and the broader enterprise, not just conceptual experimentation.

Further, while entrepreneurs typically can single-mindedly focus on the primary mission of their own company, intrapreneurs may be accountable for both the intrapreneurial venture and other organizational responsibilities.

Intrapreneurship is a synthesis of at least four basic concepts:

1. Entrepreneurship

2. Innovation

3. Excellence

4. Leadership

In my many interviews, experts expressed the critical need to understand where intrapreneurs and entrepreneurs differ.

"Entrepreneurs tend to be the maverick type," said Derek Van Nostran, longtime digital media and marketing industry veteran. "They tend to be the people who don't want bosses. . . . They want to run the show and have control. Intrapreneurs tend to be communicators, bridge builders, liaisons who want to work within a structure to move things forward but don't necessarily want to be completely on their own without that community of people to help build."[2]

Some people exemplify one of the personality types mentioned previously, and some have a combination of both.

Regardless, it is helpful to understand where you land in terms of your innate personality and your needs and interests at a given time.

While drawing important distinctions, I also want to acknowledge the similarities between intrapreneurship and entrepreneurship. Both involve taking initiative, creating value, and building teams to accomplish goals. There is no one "right" path among these two basic types and their various hybrid forms. Also, there is no absolute value judgment about choosing either basic approach. Each of us has our own journey.

While not every intrapreneur will be a successful entrepreneur (and vice versa), some people can succeed at both. Also, we evolve over time. Some entrepreneurs build a small company and then make the transition to intrapreneurial work through organic business expansion, acquisition, or other paths. Some intrapreneurs develop skills and experience that lead them to be ideally suited for an entrepreneurial path as their career progresses. Plus, we may have the requisite core skills for both, but have different levels of risk tolerance at different times.

For example, a recent college graduate with little experience and student loans may want to embark on an intrapreneurial path to start, learn, and gain financial security, and then venture out on their own later. Another person starting their career may want to take risks now in an entrepreneurial venture while obligations are relatively limited and then learn along that path. They can then become an intrapreneur later on when they have more non-professional obligations and perhaps when relative corporate stability has higher value. These same types of examples apply throughout our careers in different situations.

In any event, I advocate that we invest in self-knowledge so we can choose the best path for ourselves. And when inevitable unexpected events come up (positive, negative, or neutral), we can adjust quickly and with stronger insight into what will help us increase the probability of success and fulfillment. For those of us who identify with both paths and may have had experiences that derive from each, we are often wiser, stronger, and more effective for them.

When you know what you want to do, you can begin the process of understanding whether you're the right person to do it. And you can also discover where you really want to apply yourself.

When laying the foundation for intrapreneurship, look for the right circumstances. Securing a good fit—an organization and role in which you can see an intrapreneur succeeding—is important. If the company has no history of internal innovation, then it is usually not going to be your best environment for intrapreneurial breakthroughs. If the role offers limited chances to expand beyond delivery on known plans and operational requirements, then you will have an uphill climb as well.

Some of my most foundational intrapreneurial experiences came when I joined The Weather Channel to grow digital products and services. I arrived there after product and business development roles at 3MC and ExpoExchange—two related firms devoted to technology platforms for multiple industries including trade shows. My 3MC and ExpoExchange periods had been busy, including migration from one division to another. At one point, we shut down a product line for which I was leading product development. Then, another company bought out part of our company and we merged, but they weren't crazy about our cash flow. It was a period of change and learning for so many on our team.

I loved the process of generating new business and new ideas with this talented group of people. I wanted to keep doing the same type of work but was eager to find a chance to make more of a difference. I was looking for a big brand with more stability—one where I didn't wake up on so many days wondering about the short-term viability of the company. I found a great opportunity at The Weather Channel. It was a family-owned company with a strong history of innovation. It offered a perfect fit for my intrapreneurial aspirations.

That said, the job is just part of the assessment, and your external environment alone will not guarantee success. Start by looking within.

Know Yourself

What kind of person are you? What motivates you? What goals do you have?

You can use self-knowledge to leverage your strengths while balancing your weaknesses. We all have some of both. And when you know yourself well, you have especially valuable reference points for evaluating opportunities. Among other things, you can look around and determine if you're in a role where you've already increased the probability of success.

Getting to know yourself that well takes time and effort.

There are many paths to gain this knowledge—personal observation, diagnostics, performance reviews, conversations with coworkers and mentors, and more. Please find an approach that helps you identify your overall make-up with confidence. One type that I find highly interesting is diagnostics, which help both with personal understanding and also vocabulary to share insights about yourself with others.

For example, I've completed multiple assessments over the course of my professional career—Myers-Briggs, Birkman, Hogan, and others. These diagnostics have provided foundational insights to my approach as an intrapreneur. They illuminate the ways in which I prefer to work, the ways in which intrapreneurship will impact me, and the contours of likely team dynamics.

If you don't already have the results of one of these with reliable, relevant data and context for yourself, please consider taking one soon. You can do this either through your organization or independently, and the results will provide valuable guidance into what works best for you and how you can grow.

When you engage in an intrapreneurial project, you want to be confident that you have the right external situation and the right inner tools to meet the challenge.

Here's one way that shows up in my case: On Myers-Briggs, I'm officially an introvert—with a profile that someone later (through a Birkman) described as a "high-functioning introvert." One implication of this is that while many perceive me as highly engaged and energized, there is actually a limit to that on average compared to someone who is strongly extroverted. So, to be most effective, I need time alone to recharge and show up as my best self.

This was an important insight and connected to my innovation efforts. While I understood how many perceived me—talkative, sociable, engaged—I knew that to keep that gear available for innovation efforts, I would also need some breathing room. So, while on the road with a slate of team meetings, client discussions, or conferences to attend, I make sure to leave some time to reset and recharge whenever possible.

Over my years in business, I've reduced the number of early breakfast meetings while on the road. For good reason, they're popular ways to slip in a great discussion before other scheduled work of the day begins. However, I find that I'm usually more productive when I exercise, listen to a podcast, and/or reflect before facing challenges of the day. Also, I sometimes will start breakfasts later to allow this same space. There should be no competition to see who can be visible the most. Rather, the goal is to be most effective with the focused time we have.

I've spoken with a wide range of people on the primary personality traits of an intrapreneur and have heard many answers. We'll dive into the full list later in the chapter, but some of the most common characteristics have been the following:

- Curious

- Action-oriented

- Able to build bridges

- Risk tolerant

- Optimistic

These are the types of things that make an intrapreneur tick. Later in this chapter, I outline a broader summary of them in more detail.

Not everyone will be the same in this respect. But understanding what fuels you and what drains you is a critical step to self-awareness. When you understand your needs, you know more about how to ensure you're at full steam when necessary.

Know Your Stress Tolerance

Our varying energy needs provide a vivid example, but intrapreneurs must also understand their responses to stress, also known as stress behavior. For better or worse, in intrapreneurial ventures, there tend to be lots of demands—big goals to achieve, tight time schedules, challenges with delivery, and many opinionated people. Stress comes with the territory.

To be a successful intrapreneur, you have to understand your own tolerance for the experience. Now, of course, it's nice when things go exactly as planned. Fortunately, the teams that I've worked with have had many experiences with award-winning achievements and broad impact. But things don't always go swimmingly.

Consider this scenario: You're working on an innovative new product and (for reasons you can't control) you're asked to debut that service much earlier than you would have liked. Under this unplanned stress test, major bugs emerge, and you and your team must scramble to address them in real time and in the full spotlight of public view. I've been through this. Many other intrapreneurs have been through this too. When you innovate from within the walls of a larger organization, you don't always get to decide when and how your work will unfold and face wider scrutiny.

These things happen. And that's a good reason to understand your stress tolerance. Along with exposure to unpredictable outcomes as an organization grows, intrapreneurs also take on career risk. They sometimes need to be prepared to move from one role to another in the organization, even one that differs greatly from their first choice.

As simple as these statements are, they also convey the fundamental truth associated with this type of work. Of course, no role is risk-free. But in a corporation where everyone naturally has some exposure to changes in the internal and external environment, the intrapreneur reaches for an additional helping. Intrapreneurship involves elevated risk—with lots of upside and also a plateload of challenges—compared to many other roles in larger organizations. It is best to accept this dynamic if you are going to plunge in with full heart and mind. The most successful intrapreneurs I've seen and heard from accept elevated career risk as a cost of doing this type of business. Be ready to accept and embrace it even as you welcome the satisfaction, fulfillment, and/or recognition that come with big accomplishments. Regardless of the outcome, this mindset always gives you the freedom to act in the best interests of the business versus primarily protecting your own. You will have bumps, bruises, and disappointments as an intrapreneur. Keep your focus on the organizational mission and you stand a better chance of excelling and growing value over time. And all that said, you still have the resources of the organization behind you.

Juan Andrés Muñoz, an experienced intrapreneur who was a key builder of CNN en Español, describes the personality in more detail. "I think there's a very specific type of person that will want to be an intrapreneur," he said. This is an individual with all the skills and experience to be an entrepreneur but the commitment and the team orientation to meld creativity with the resources of a big firm. He describes the company infrastructure as a bonus, not a hindrance. That's the hybrid. If working for a company gives you the safety net to experiment and be daring, he indicates that this is how many great ideas come to life.[3]

Hold Fast to Your Principles

There's another inner conversation an intrapreneur must have, and that's around principles. We all have principles that guide us—inner reference points that help us navigate complicated moments. Regardless of your role, your principles will matter as you engage in the daily work of running a business. Some decisions and principles are very clear conceptually, even if not always easy in practice. They include the way you treat colleagues and employees, your commitment to delivering for customers, and your sense of personal integrity when you give your word.

Organizations define and disseminate corporate principles to provide instruction and clarity to a wide swath of employees. Ideally, a team develops these concepts together. When tackled thoughtfully, this valuable exercise involving vision (and/or mission), goals, and values can provide extra octane to fuel your business, a turbocharger of sorts that facilitates moving from good to great.

When you enter the space of intrapreneurship, decision-making can get more complicated. Now, instead of simply following the corporate guidelines for known situations, you push into new territory. There can be a strong sense of your innovative effort also involving "special circumstances" at times—ones that require a large degree of discretion. In these critical moments, the most successful intrapreneurs must be confident and comfortable both in their alignment with requirements of the broader organization and also in their personally held principles.

Thankfully, many of us have had a chance to work in organizations that consistently live up to high standards and have not faced a meaningful ethical quandary. Unfortunately, many others have been in situations in which we've been asked (or thought we were expected) to cross an ethical line. Perhaps we were instructed to fill out an expense report or time sheet in a way that didn't reflect the facts. Perhaps we were counseled to hide information from a client or misrepresent ourselves in a sales pitch. Often these requests seem small, even trivial. If this happens, they tend to be presented as "just the way things are done." These types of challenges can involve clear and simple ethical dimensions like statements of fact, and they can also blur into gray areas.

In any event, it's important to understand your principles clearly. From my perspective, one of these should be unquestionable integrity. Dedicate yourself early to the pursuit of this standard and make it where your ethical lines are drawn. The request to compromise these principles may come suddenly and without warning. When you're secure in your own position, you won't hesitate or waffle. You'll know your answer. Some readers of this book will be at the beginning of their careers. Especially for these promising leaders, I want to help you prepare for the possibility that you will run into this type of situation and provide you with a fire extinguisher for it in advance. I also hope you never need to use it.

When working with a lot of different people across a range of organizations, the potential remains for ethical concerns. Navigating these can be especially difficult for an intrapreneur who is already trying to move mountains. Do not create an unnecessary obstacle for yourself by indiscretion in this area. At a minimum, a misstep can erode trust and create concerns that undermine your effectiveness over time. In some cases, and even if you are otherwise performing, it can cost you your job.

I've been exposed to more than one of these challenges in my career. I came in with a simple mindset—that honesty would consistently anchor conversations and relationships as the primary default position. So I was deeply concerned when coworkers and I were asked at several points by people in leadership (people we looked up to) to do something we believed was not ethical. Also, others have come to me for coaching when facing similar issues.

Expense reports present one type of situation to watch for. I'm going to highlight this because it can seem so small, so relatively benign. And yet sometimes small things send big signals. And big signals can reveal aspects of a company's culture or an environment you'll want to avoid.

At least twice in my career, I've been asked to misrepresent information on an expense report. For example, this can take the form of a fabricated business purpose that is made up to cover a non-business activity, or extra people on the attendee list for a meal to meet internal expense report criteria. I know other people who have experienced this as well. In each case, I've flatly declined to do it, saying I'm not comfortable saying something that I know isn't true. And in general, it didn't end there. The follow-on goes something like this: "It's no big deal," or "Everybody does it," or "Come on, be a team player." And when you hear this, please know this is not the case. This is not small, everybody doesn't do it, and a team player protects the ethics of the organization.

On the surface, this type of situation is trivial compared to intentional and massive fraud in a company like Enron or Theranos. Yet in my view, it can lead to much bigger failure over time. The fracturing of trust, as well as danger signs, appears in things large and small. So, large or small, just don't do it.

The best way to face this challenge is to dedicate yourself to the highest ethical standards, and then act accordingly. You may get pushback when you take an unpopular position. Often, ethical compromises are suggested to "keep the peace," "not rock the boat," or "avoid conflict." And that can sound very attractive in the moment. But principles are designed to guide you not just in easy times, but also in difficult ones. If this is an isolated incident, then you can actually uphold the values of the culture by being honest and setting an example that others will follow to improve your environment. And if it isn't isolated, then consider looking for another role—soon.

When you're exploring new territory and pushing for innovation, there will be times when you get pushback, and others when you are encouraged to do something in a new, creative—perhaps unsanctioned—way. When that happens, you need to be clear on where your own principles stand and what principles are held by the team overall. You may find your values are in sync with the new demand. Or you may realize there's a conflict. Either way, the sooner you understand the issue, the quicker you can act to resolve it.

I've long operated in business with three guiding principles:

- Do the right thing
- Serve our customers
- Move forward

I follow these principles intentionally and keep them in mind consistently. When facing a decision—either individually or as part of a team—these provide a framework with which to make a call and feel confident in it. They don't guarantee perfection (that's not possible). Rather, I simply strive to achieve them always. Sometimes this means stumbling, sometimes implementing imperfectly, but always returning. And always working to make it right where I—or our team—missed something along the way. These types of guidelines help in the many ambiguous, uncertain, and time-critical situations when the team assesses and aligns based on them. These principles also provide clarity for action and thinking with the occasional negative pushback you may receive from someone who chooses to deviate from them.

Understanding your principles can help you feel confident in decisions in the moment, and they also serve as a litmus test when trying to understand your potential for intrapreneurial success in any one place.

In my career, most people have exhibited high integrity in thought and actions. The rare exception has underscored the value of consistent principles. That said, unethical bosses do exist in some companies. If you find one and have principles that differ from those of your superior, you need to understand that this boss probably won't change. Some things like skills are more malleable; character is less so.

This observation extends to your comfort with ambiguity and risk. If you lead teams and drive innovation in a corporate setting, you may have already advanced to a senior level within the company. It also stands to reason that your colleagues and bosses are generally not new to the business. They come to their work with experiences and decisions that have shaped them and led them to their current roles. They are who they are, and they have often built a track record of success on their finely honed processes. You typically are not going to get far if you challenge those processes. When you see the clash of principles or over-all style in a corporate setting, your innovation upside is likely limited. You probably need to find a new role within the orga-nization, or a new employer. I've seen this enough to know that unless the boss leaves before you do, you're going to continue to be unhappy with this arrangement until you find another place to apply your skills.

Can You Lead Self-Care?

Finally, as you prepare for the experience of intrapreneurship, consider your ability to promote self-care. This refers to you and to the mandate you will bring to an intrapreneurial team. Intrapreneurship is demanding. It requires energy and commit-ment to drive change that differs from the basic descriptions of a more established corporate role.

Do you understand your own needs around self-care? Can

you extend that perspective to an intrapreneurial team? And if we're really achieving at a high level and lifting people up, can you extend that so that you model it with family and friends? After all, the work environment and experiences outside of work connect in important and interdependent ways whether we like it or not.

Lots of jobs place heavy demands on people, so intrapreneurship doesn't hold that distinction alone. However, intrapreneurship often requires so much effort—to feed the various lions and tigers and bears in your company—that you're left with very little energy to take care of yourself.

About the time that our first child arrived, someone reminded us as new parents to "put your own oxygen mask on first." This is an often-used analogy, spun off from the routine instructions from the flight crew to airline passengers, and it may seem like a cliché. But it's very important to raise at this point in our discussion. Because when talking about the personality traits of an intrapreneur, many of my interviews turned up the same language: intrapreneurs are helpers.

Quincy Johnson, a media technology executive with particular depth in global content platforms, sees the helper thread in his own process. "I always try to establish myself as a person that's here to help and to help people. I interact with people and solve problems, and it's great because a lot of times you build trust with others, and then they're willing to share insights and help you out when you need help."[4]

Doug Busk, a mobile industry innovator and thought leader, used very similar language when I talked with him about intrapreneurs and their motivations. "What I've come to realize is it's not so much about, 'oh, I like a paycheck and risk profile.' It's that intrapreneurs like helping people. The more people they're surrounded by, the more people they can help, the better. And they aren't driven by dollars. They might be driven by visibility, but they're not driven by vanity."[5]

Being a helper is a good thing. But it's also a reminder to keep that oxygen mask metaphor in mind. You can't serve others as well if you're depleted, especially over a long time. Now, all of us go through periods when we're running on fumes—at home, at work, in the community, and beyond. Remember on your own behalf (because you can't always count on others to remind you) that you can only go on so long without taking care of yourself.

Sometimes, it manifests as a five-minute break to practice mindfulness or listen to some of your favorite music. Sometimes, it's a day off to focus on other interests. Maybe you make a bigger commitment like taking a vacation when practical. Maybe it's having a salad instead of a burger. Or taking time to call and connect with a friend for a few minutes, instead of immediately going to the next thing on the to-do list. The range of options is nearly endless. However, for sure, my experience is that you need to put boundaries on your time—not just to keep things in balance but also to preserve your ability to perform at a sustainably high level. I keep this concept top of mind in my own work and when I'm leading a team.

Here's an example:

Many leaders face times of particularly concentrated demands at work, and I've seen a fair number of those too. In one case, our team was in the middle of both a business transformation and also a full cross-section of connected needs within our teams and in the broader marketplace. Everyone felt it intensely. We had new people doing new things, sometimes in new roles. At times, people worked late on workdays and then again late on weekends, and it all seemed essential. Emotions ran high.

We were clearly in an intrapreneurial situation. We were all still employees, working on our company projects related to ongoing daily business operations and committed to the success of the firm. But we were also engaged in a rapid process of innovation. To adapt, we had to reinvent many of our business practices. But we also experienced a crash course for leaders on how to innovate within the walls of a company. You are still an employee. Yet you are engaged in a creative endeavor that may change everything. You are innovating, whether you want to or not.

Because innovation demands in this area grew rapidly, few had the luxury of stopping to consider deeply how it might impact us all as human beings. Happiness in our jobs could seem secondary, given the needs to care for the business and the team. Yet, to lead innovation effectively within the walls of a company, you should understand your self-care needs and assist others in the process of understanding their own.

To respond to this situation, our leadership team decided to implement time boundaries. Outside of team members who worked nontraditional hours, no emails or other communication would be sent after a specific time on weekdays. No emails on weekends. We acknowledged in these new guidelines that emergencies would arise. But we set that standard high, too. Marking something off a to-do list was not an emergency. Checking in or prepping for a future engagement or meeting was not an emergency. In a world where "emergency" sometimes seemed to be the default position, we broke new ground and created rules on how we would use the term in our operation. We had the guidelines to talk the talk, and then the results depended on the degree to which we walked the walk, together.

It was important for us to see our human selves and our human needs, even in the midst of a very demanding business situation. As intrapreneurs, even though we had not sought the role in this particular case, we wanted to help and innovate. At the same time, this situation was uniquely and powerfully stressful. We needed to remember our own self-care priorities alongside our intrapreneurial drive.

We implemented this process change in our leadership team, then in other parts of the company. Our field leaders started implementing similar policies. The innovation took hold and others embraced it as well. The key: we took control of our own destiny and reduced exposure to burnout, thereby increasing our ability to achieve the goals of serving our customers and supporting our teammates.

Focus on Contribution

As you engage in this inner evaluation, use your time to focus your thinking. Are you focused on contribution, and how are you focused on it inside your company? Management thinker Peter Drucker recognized that understanding where you can make a contribution is one of the most important steps to personal excellence. This is a critical guideline for the intrapreneur.

This effort differs in scope and responsibility from that of a typical entrepreneur. Entrepreneurs can often focus single-mindedly on goals where their primary responsibilities for daily work are synonymous with the needs of the company overall. That's all part of the entrepreneurial process. But the intrapreneur has a different situation in some respects, bound up in contributing to the broader organization while also being responsible for a narrower primary mandate. Also, the intrapreneur may have to navigate through broad corporate policies that are designed for more mature businesses, before implementing certain types of changes.

While the entrepreneur can anchor mainly in the entrepreneurial world, the intrapreneur must be able to toggle back and forth fluidly between being an unconventional thinker and rule follower. Keith Wilmot, former leader of the innovation hub for a major packaged goods company and founder of a company that fosters corporate innovation, compares this capability to being able to speak multiple languages.

"An entrepreneur doesn't have to be bilingual. An entrepreneur can go out and speak his language or her language and launch a new something. An intrapreneur must have that chameleon ability. The ability to be multilingual and dexterous inside of a company," he said.[6] That's what's necessary to operate effectively, from his perspective.

As you begin your process of innovation and intrapreneurship, focus your thinking on how you contribute best to the organization.

This focus can be a bigger mental leap than it appears. Other factors compete for attention. When you embark on an intrapreneurial effort, it's easy to get caught up in other questions. How long will it take? How difficult will it be to accomplish? How robust and advanced is the technology involved? How visible will it be? How will this affect my career? Other topics may divert the intrapreneur as well. When advancing a discussion about an intrapreneurial idea, they will encounter various considerations like resource availability and allocation, office politics, ownership at multiple levels, priorities, and more.

So, when you're engaged in your mental inventory, ask yourself: Are these goals what we'll be most proud of when we're finished? Do these approaches best fuel the fire to attain the highest success, in line with our principles? And first and foremost, am I focused on contribution?

Now here's where it gets even more interesting: contribution does not exist in a vacuum. Multiple other factors—including the right people in the right places, technology, communication, and securing support—matter. They matter a lot. For the purposes of broader success, continue to ask how your work contributes to the organization overall. By the way, this mindset inherently helps place the good of the organization ahead of what's best for you personally or your team alone. Sometimes you have to sacrifice your good for what's best for the broader organization, although both considerations align much of the time. And this approach, in turn, necessitates a service mentality in which you subordinate yourself to the broader organization and team in a balance that benefits from self-knowledge and experience.

Documenting how you will contribute to the broader organization in your prep work puts you in the right mental space to engage in innovation while maintaining your positive relationship with your corporate employer. It keeps your vision focused ahead on what's good for the organization and even the industry. When, later down the road, you hit legitimate concerns and hurdles to your efforts, the ability to refer directly to your contribution to the organization will be invaluable. It will underscore the worth of your innovation.

The Value of Inner Work

It may feel strange to engage in a process of soul-searching in a corporate setting. In many cases, the business world doesn't ask us how we feel, how we're doing emotionally, what would make us happier, more secure, and more engaged.

But lack of consistent focus on these issues at a corporate level doesn't decrease their importance. And self-knowledge underpins the process of innovation and intrapreneurship. When you set out on a groundbreaking, line-crossing, and norm-busting venture, you will naturally encounter those who prefer the status quo. You will be confronted with many forms of the word "no." You'll be told that can't happen in our industry, the board won't approve it, the shareholders won't see the value, and the brass will never go along. Change discussions frequently meet these types of resistance.

For that reason, the innovation leader must be ready for both sustained collaborative effort and challenges—whatever these may be. It may be a flawed technology platform or an ethical dilemma or a pandemic. If you intend to put yourself into this role, lead change, and innovate, you'll need to be ready—inside and out—for the tasks at hand.

Here's how Joe Fiveash, an experienced digital media executive who has created some of the most lasting services, teams, and relationships in the news and information space, put it: "I think you have to try it and see if you like it. And understand that it comes with stress and discomfort. You may find it's not for you. But for some people, once you've tasted it, nothing else is satisfying."[7]

Who you are will figure significantly in the success of your innovation.

Know that and you're on the way to your successful outcome.

Overall, some primary characteristics of successful intrapreneurs have emerged through my experience and interviews. Here's a summary:

1. **Curious.** It is essential for a superior intrapreneur to have a sense of curiosity and to apply learning from a wide range of sources and experiences.

2. **Action-Oriented.** An intrapreneur must take action. One of the primary characteristics of intrapreneurs is that they make things happen that truly add value.

3. **Able to Build Bridges.** All superior intrapreneurs have this capability. It is one of the things that can distinguish the intrapreneur from the entrepreneur, especially in a large and collaborative organization.

4. **Risk Tolerant.** Risk tolerance is necessary to differentiate the intrapreneur from the talented person who is more comfortable with predictability and routine. An intrapreneur values challenge, opportunity, and achievement over stability.

5. **Optimistic.** An intrapreneur exudes optimism. Not just any kind, but grounded optimism, supported by relevant knowledge and a commitment to addressing practical needs while pursuing audacious, innovative goals. An intrapreneur practices possibility thinking. An intrapreneur sees and finds opportunities, and then pursues them with an expectation of an even brighter future. They do it in an uplifting way that helps other people share that vision for the future too.

6. **Hard-working.** Intrapreneurship requires tremendous effort. It takes time to develop the idea, communicate, and build in so many ways. Therefore, it requires a sustained work ethic to deliver on the opportunity. Without this trait, all the other ones diminish by a large margin.

7. **Adaptable.** An intrapreneur needs to be able to adapt to an organizational environment, and as market conditions change. This is not the same as resilience—sometimes it's incremental and adjusting to positive change.

8. **Versatile with Communications.** An intrapreneur should have a range of communication skills, from listening well to sharing a vision to building relationships. This capability carries a particular premium due to the range of audiences involved.

9. **Resilient.** An intrapreneur will have setbacks. They get used to it and then bounce back. They develop the ability to navigate through the inevitable highs and lows of the journey with more emotional maturity and sustained focus on the goals.

10. **Insightful.** One of the most important capabilities of an intrapreneur is to see opportunities that some others don't, and to understand how to realize their potential.

11. **Ethical.** Integrity matters in all aspects of life. An intrapreneur requires credibility and trust for sustained success. Some of this is built by accomplishing things, some by truth-telling and promise-keeping, and some manifests simply as a way of being.

12. **Respectful.** Important for many reasons, respect takes particular forms for the intrapreneur. One of those, of course, is respect for other people—different types of people in different roles. Another is respect for the organization—its history, the best parts of its culture, and the other divisions (some of which generally provide the cash flow for intrapreneurial success, at least earlier on).

13. **Different.** While respecting people and the organization, you also can achieve best when looking at the world a little differently, and then bringing your views to bear to benefit customers, the team, and the organization.

14. **Culturally Aware.** Intrapreneurs are willing to push for change. And they do it in an environment where there are financial, operational, and cultural boundaries. Understanding and working within these makes a big difference for the most successful intrapreneurs.

15. **Humble.** Humility plays an important role in multiple dimensions and development stages of an initiative. It's important early on, when you may feel that you have a good idea that doesn't have buy-in yet. It's important later, when you have a big success, to share the benefits with

those around you. It's important in a range of discussions and situations at every stage of the journey. When leavened with self-confidence in a healthy balance, retaining humility enables an intrapreneur to achieve more.

16. **Courageous.** Naturally, the intrapreneur faces uncertainty, risk of failure, and challenging discussions at various turns along the way. You must practice courage in combination with other traits to achieve goals while recognizing that you and your team are part of a much larger ecosystem.

The right combination of traits in the previous list makes for the most successful intrapreneurs. Yes, this is a lot—and it's a reason that superior intrapreneurship adds such high value to an organization.

This list can be turned into an evaluation to assess fit with intrapreneurship. There are some things that do not differentiate intrapreneurs, too.

- **Introversion and extroversion.** People can be either and succeed.

- **Financial or business knowledge, beyond a basic threshold.** Some intrapreneurs have a lot and some have a little—this can generally be addressed with others on the team.

- **Personal or venture capital.** Unlike entrepreneurs, anyone with the skills has the opportunity to build a venture without funding the venture themselves or personally raising capital outside of their organization.

- **A company's geographical location.** Intrapreneurs can be successful anywhere there is a strong organization that provides a welcoming home—or where they can be connected to one. This is true from large cities to small towns around the world.

- **Depth of technology knowledge.** Intrapreneurs range from PhDs to philosophy majors to people who chose not to go to college. This discipline is accessible for anyone who has the requisite other characteristics.

Various people have commented on the ideal mix of these traits. Aidoo Osei, leader of innovation at a global financial technology company, describes the preferred combination of intrapreneurial characteristics in this way:

It requires a mix of critical skills. Typically, an intrapreneur is going to be a person who's an integrative thinker, someone able to take multiple pieces of data, synthesize that data, and tell a story about what it means. Whether data is quantitative or qualitative or maybe a narrative story, an intrapreneur has to be a storyteller in some way, form, or fashion. That means they have to be a great communicator. They have to have the relationships and abilities to be persuasive. The other thing is they have to have a unique perspective on things. You've got to be able to look at the world a little bit differently. And maybe they're not original ideas, but maybe you're applying things from another industry to your industry in a novel way. The best intrapreneurs are good connectors.[8]

While the specific set of intrapreneurial capabilities may vary by person, I want to pick up on a key aspect of Aidoo's experience-based observations: the best intrapreneurs apply a specific mix of skills in a multifaceted environment. A larger organization almost by definition requires multiple skills to lead effectively across organizational boundaries, across a range of people, and in the context of a company's strategic needs. The best intrapreneurs will combine their own talents with integrative thinking and action orientation to add value to the enterprise and the people associated with it. The time to do your inner work—to know yourself and your capabilities—is now.

Chapter Summary

This chapter asks the intrapreneur to begin with a process of introspection to evaluate their likely fit in the context of intrapreneurial dynamics and needs.

- Understand your own motivations, style, and goals.

- Develop and express your personal principles. Ideally, write them down.

- Understand the key characteristics of successful intrapreneurs, and what is not required.

- Commit to a focus on contribution.

- Compare your own capabilities and aspirations with intrapreneurial needs.

- Combine the preceding to lay a solid foundation for the exciting road ahead!

CHAPTER 2

SCAN FOR OPPORTUNITY

Intrapreneurs are not people who let grass grow under their feet.

These are individuals who get an idea and are typically raring to go, go, go! Sometimes they want to start testing, other times they advocate for building prototypes, still other times they want to run ideas by prospective customers. Sometimes they're ready to roll out implementation, or maybe they just want to brainstorm further with trusted coworkers. In any event, the experience is incomplete without true, meaningful action. It's the reason having an "action orientation" is one of the key traits of an intrapreneur. I've met a lot of successful intrapreneurs, and they are all action-oriented.

And for that reason, this next bit of advice may seem somewhat daunting.

The idea that your first steps on a promising concept may be measured and thoughtful will not always be met with enthusiasm. After all, didn't we just spend Chapter 1 doing all the internal work to prepare for the intrapreneurial adventure?

Yes, in fact, we did. But that still brings us to a moment filled with a different sort of action—action that is as mental as it is physical. Picture shoppers entering the department store during the holidays looking for a special gift and with many options before them. Do they usually walk through the door and grab the first thing they see? Of course not. Shoppers don't want just any old gifts. They want the best gifts—ones that are thoughtful, ones that can be used and enjoyed, and ones that provide special value for the receiver.

Expand the landscape a bit and imagine an explorer, moving forward through uncharted territory. The explorer doesn't simply want *a* route forward. The explorer wants the *best* route ahead.

While a holiday shopper or explorer can work from intuition, an intrapreneur has additional tools at their disposal. Familiar business practices can be leveraged early on to create a strong start for an intrapreneurial project. In this chapter, we review the best practices when it comes to scanning for an intrapreneurial opportunity. You may feel like you already have your best idea, but this chapter discusses the thoughtful examination that will ensure that you're making the optimal decision. In the end, you may decide your first idea is exactly right. You may tweak it to be its very best. Or, upon examining the landscape of your market more closely in the context of your company's strategy, you may determine that an entirely different idea makes more sense. Ideally, that's not the kind of realization you want to have far down the path. It's one that you want to have earlier in the process. You need to combine data, reflection, analysis, and instinct to chart the best course.

Assess the External Marketplace and Internal Environment

In your intrapreneurial zeal to build the app or find the partnership or secure the resources, you may feel the urge to skip over your critical first steps: assessing the external marketplace and internal environment. How ready is each for your initiative? The business landscape abounds with ideas that have arrived before or after their times. Also, many concepts that held great promise have withered in an organization that did not value them at the time they most needed to develop. So, what level of need or interest will customers have, and how will they respond if you germinate it in-house? Internally, how does the idea align with the strategic needs, capabilities, and priorities of your organization? You should understand your company's overall strategy and align your efforts with it—ideally with the early support of senior leaders.

Marie Quintero-Johnson, longtime beverage industry leader and former head of global corporate development at Coca-Cola, sets the stage for this important area of opportunity selection. She observes:

> I think, particularly in big corporations, that everything
> has to be grounded in a strategy. And so, if you have a

one-, three-, five-year strategy, whatever the term may be, intrapreneurship should be prioritized based on and in service of the strategy. And that's not to say that you can't come up with something new that you didn't know or that you didn't know that somebody needed. But I would say that 90 percent of intrapreneurship should be in the service of strategy, and that is what drives prioritization and resource allocation. This is so critical, not only for financial resource allocation, but people and mind space are super important. So, for me, it all starts with strategy and prioritization.[1]

Tom Daly, digital marketing innovator in consumer packaged goods and services who "turns big ships in small spaces," gives this advice to the potential intrapreneur: look for the ideas that will add speed to what's already happening within the walls of the firm.

"The better ideas are the ones that get you where you want to go, faster," he says.[2] When you're working for a big company, there may be markets and platforms at which you will likely eventually end up, but a great intrapreneurial idea can jumpstart that evolution. When you can get to where you want to go, but faster, you disrupt the existing rhythms of an organization. You make your competitors reactive—as opposed to your company having to be reactive. When you're the one reacting, some of your choices are gone.

Michael Britt at Southern Telecom highlighted to me how power provider Southern Company identified telecommunications as a logical way to expand its business, finding new uses for strategic assets with historical roots.[3] At the same time, Jim Trupiano, who has also worked in an innovation center at parent company Southern Company, pointed out that renewable energy is now coming on strong with growth opportunities that also benefit the environment.[4] In these cases, diverse opportunities have emerged at different stages of market evolution. While these innovative leaders point out that new ideas represent less than one percent of the revenue opportunity at large companies like theirs early on, they also understand that some emerging businesses will be the primary growth drivers of the future—and have made major progress in realizing their potential already.

As you scan the landscape, building on existing strengths is one way to link to strategy, and delving deeper into areas that are currently less promising will present opportunities as well.

Look for a neglected part of your company's portfolio, suggests Craig Kirkland, mobile industry executive and innovator with expertise in wireless carriers, media, financial services, and research. "Sometimes the opportunity will emerge organically, perhaps in a regular problem-solving session. Or maybe you take an insight from an old job and apply it to a new company. These are the ways you can spot opportunities," he says.[5] The space you seek may be right in front of you.

Quint Studer, a highly successful healthcare executive, entrepreneur, and author, learned early that the opportunities may be inside the organization. He tells a story from growing up that left a lasting impression.

An intrapreneur can do quite well. I consider my father one. He worked at Electro-Motive, which was a division of General Motors, in a plant that made diesel engines for trains. He was a diesel mechanic. They had a suggestion program, and my dad might have led all of Electro-Motive on approved suggestions. Anyone who had a suggestion approved got a small amount of dollars, but they also got a certificate and they were named in the newsletter. Our basement walls were covered with my dad's suggestions on how to make the process better, how to make the engine better.

In fact, it got to the point when an engine would break down, they would send him to the engine because it was cheaper to do that than to bring the engine back to Chicago. So, he was an intrapreneur. He probably could have taken these tools and processes and started his own diesel mechanic consulting company. He probably could have gone to General Motors and said, "Why don't you hire me as a consultant to do this?" But he had this fear of going from getting a paycheck and a pension and insurance to being completely at risk, and that was something that he just couldn't handle.

Organizations should love intrapreneurs because they're the people that are pushing you to be better. They're the "push people" who are coming up with ideas. They're the people who are coming up with ways to improve processes. And it takes some companies a while to understand their value. They might think, well gee, this person's always trying to make us better, this person's complaining, this person doesn't like us. That's not true at all. This person just wants the organization to be better.[6]

Quint carried that mindset through to his own work. A good intrapreneur can make a big difference, he learned. "If you look at a big company, a little change can be hundreds of thousands of dollars," he says. The trick is to scan internally for the right opportunity.

Quint offered another example from his experience. He was part of the leadership team at a small hospital when his team fielded a survey to see how customers perceived the institution's improvements in technology.

> I was excited when I became a department director and got business cards. I was in charge of planning and marketing and business development. And we did a Gallup survey that said people thought we were promoting that we care. And it came out that people knew we care, they just didn't think we knew what we were doing, because we were a small hospital. So they said, well, what people want to know is do you have the scale, do you have the technology, and do you care? So, I created tools that went on every computer to remind us what to say. Every time we talked to somebody, we started off with the skill and talked about the technology. Then we said we care.

That was an especially memorable intrapreneurial opportunity for Quint. The new software ensured that the hospital employee, in every communication with a customer, would start off the conversation by emphasizing the medical expertise and technological capabilities. It was a new tool for the company and one that opened up improvements that would otherwise not have been realized.

So, is your idea one that will secure an edge for your company? Let's look at how to evaluate this.

Assessing the marketplace is the first step for many people who are hoping to launch a new product or service or exploring a strategic idea. This process appears for both intrapreneurs and entrepreneurs. Both benefit from understanding the reception that awaits their idea in the marketplace. But intrapreneurs often have an edge at this stage. While the entrepreneur may need to rely on gut instinct and some limited research—they'll often lack the resources to afford much else—many intrapreneurs have resources inside the enterprise walls that yield definitive information on the topic of marketplace readiness.

Bill Burke, a media executive who led multiple cable TV networks including Turner Classic Movies, TBS, and The Weather Channel, describes his arrival at Turner Broadcasting:

> When I got the tour of the Techwood mansion right by Georgia Tech, they were showing me, here's the little control room for TNT, and here's the one for TBS, and then there are three or four empty ones. I said, "What are those?" And they said, "Those are for the next networks we're going to launch." And I said, "Oh, what networks are those?" and they said, "We don't know yet, but we're going to do it." I got that tour in July. Actually, they had announced that the launch of the Cartoon Network would be that following October. Then, little did I know I was about to develop a business plan for Turner Classic Movies, which launched less than two years later. And

TNT Latin America and Cartoon Latin America; they were full within three years.[7]

Clayton Christensen, author of *The Innovator's Dilemma*, identified types of resources including people, equipment, technology, product designs, brands, information, cash, and relationships with suppliers, distributors, and customers.[8] Information is one thing that may be available in abundance and does not require investment in many cases—the investment often comes later. On the topic of data and insight, let's look at a few potential data resources the intrapreneur will have at hand:

- **Internal data on your current business.** A large enterprise typically has information in abundance. Customer data is routinely gathered and sorted for trends and guidance. What can the available customer data tell you about the idea you're now forming? Can you access the data and sort it for your own view of the marketplace—one that signals the readiness of the customer base for your new concept? When I was at The Weather Channel, we referred to a treasure trove of data constantly. It represented a body of knowledge related to people interested in weather. From that starting point, the data could be sorted to understand all sorts of other things. We could break it down into segments such as basic, daily weather info (hot, cold, wet, dry); severe weather for specific and sometimes life-saving situations; and tailored weather information for specific lifestyle and health activities. So, in addition to daily and event-based needs, you could look at smaller slices of the information regarding pollen, skiing, or spring planting. The potential avenues for exploration were numerous. So much of the data was already within our walls. An intrapreneur with an idea for a service focused on specific segments would often have access to lots of information to contribute to a thoughtful opportunity evaluation. One note: This type of data mining and analysis clearly has limitations if you intend to serve customers in segments that differ from your current business. It can also distract if you are creating something wholly new that looks more like Ford's Model T or the Apple iPhone, where current customer behaviors differ fundamentally from future ones. However—and this is the important point—your commitment to delivering something truly innovative should not be used as an excuse to shirk the task of viewing what you already do have. Available data will often make even the most groundbreaking idea better.

- **Partner data.** If your team is gathering data in-house, you can bet that your current partners are doing it as well. What do they know that will contribute to your opportunity evaluation process? Business partners come in all shapes and sizes. A media company such as The Weather Channel had partners that focused on needs from technology to advertising and far beyond. A manufacturer will have suppliers and shipping partners. A retailer will have a wholesaler, an advertising firm, and a staffing provider. Partners will have data pertaining to their current work with you and information that may come from other parts of their business. Connecting with them may reveal new sources of data you had not previously considered.

- **Third-party research.** Anyone can hire a firm to conduct outside research. But many intrapreneurs (vs. entrepreneurs) will have access to more resources to make that happen. Accessing third-party research is a critical step for intrapreneurs since it provides unbiased reference material for the new concept. It's an area in which an intrapreneur should be open-minded and also proceed judiciously. Plenty of consulting firms will provide valuable services, and some can make business-changing contributions. When contracting for third-party research, be sure you know what you're getting into so that the results contribute directly to your venture in meaningful ways, and the benefits justify the bill.

Then, put that information to the test. Joshua Sommer, innovator, inventor, intrapreneur, and entrepreneur who has overseen the growth of many businesses in larger organizations, offers this checklist:[9]

1. Quantify the customer problem.
2. Frame the market and the size of the opportunity.
3. Assess the space: Are there other providers in it? Is it whitespace where you're inventing and defining the world? Or fragmented spaces with people running around in it but they don't have the scale and size of a corporation?

4. Do you have the right to play? Is it in service of what the wider corporation is trying to accomplish?

5. Is it a sustainable opportunity?

When evaluating opportunities, it's important for the intrapreneur to be aware of the role of relationships in data sharing. You may be reaching beyond the bounds of your regular work scope to investigate and formulate an innovative idea. You also may be reaching into functional territory that is not traditionally your own. To do this successfully, relationship awareness emerges as key. You want to be able to access the information—internally, with partners, and even with outside firms—without getting anyone in your current enterprise bent out of shape.

Along with your own initiative and overall relationships, one of your best avenues for conducting productive research is a supportive boss. If your boss is a strong advocate for you and intrapreneurship in general, that's often your first and best stop. That individual clears the way for your data-gathering process. This senior individual can send an email or make a call to the guardian of the data essentially saying: "I would appreciate you helping my intrapreneur. Please call me if you have any questions." With that kind of introduction, you are likely to get what you need. You may still encounter barriers. (By the way, obstruction happens in just about any company. Delay happens. Marginalization happens, too, in a world where you're the diminutive preschooler and another part of the business is the figurative teenager, adult, or grandparent.) But the support from a higher-up is a huge boost.

Now, let's suppose that best case scenario is not at your disposal. For whatever reason, you can't work with your boss to open the data vault. In this situation, preexisting company relationships provide a key to advancing your project. You may not know the senior leader, but you may have relationships with others in the department—others who can help you explore the data options and put you in front of the right decision-makers.

In many cases, these relationships can't be forged as easily on the fly with a "just in time" approach. Where practical, reach out and connect with others in the company long before you need them to do you a favor or support your project. Ongoing relationship-building throughout the organization should be part of your approach. The day will come when you have a great idea for an intrapreneurial effort—but you really need to see inside the data of department X. If you already know someone, have talked to someone, are water cooler (or virtual catch-up) pals with someone in department X, you're moving forward. If you've never had a conversation with anyone in department X before, the path to trust and open sharing can be much more difficult. You may still pull it off, but it can take more time and explanation than would otherwise be the case.

A note for people who have recently joined a team or company: you're often at a major disadvantage here in the relationship department compared with people who have longer tenure. The degree to which this newbie situation presents a challenge is directly proportional to the emphasis that your company puts on longstanding relationships to get things done. If that's the case and you're new, most of your relationships will typically be new as well. That's a fact, so get used to it. However, new team members can also conduct an initiative such as a listening tour to learn from many people in a relatively short time. When you approach it that way, you have the opportunity to engage your new colleagues quickly to help in your own acceleration, including navigation inside the company.

It helps to have an environment that values ideas from anywhere within the organization. Jim DiAndreth, a long-time veteran of innovation and growth ventures, underscores the benefits of valuing ideas from a wide range of people, as well as an environment that systematically channels ideas into action. As an innovation leader at the global paper and construction materials giant Georgia-Pacific, he observes, "We're always focused on growth and how to increase the value of the company. We encourage a bottoms-up approach to unleash creativity, initiative, and talents of the employees. We're expecting them to bring forward their ideas and to lead opportunities in that kind of dimension."[10]

Chris Walters, a successful executive who has led innovative growth businesses in companies from Bloomberg to The Weather Channel to Avantax, noted that there are two primary types of innovation in his experience: bigger bets with devoted teams and resources, and smaller incremental improvements that can also add substantial value with less time and investment. He made an additional observation that aligns well with the earlier story from Quint Studer about ongoing innovation. Walters noted, "The question we want the entire organization focused on is very simple: how do we actually get better at literally everything we do, how can we make progress faster, be more efficient and effective, with a focus on delighting our clients? It's a simpler, more broadly understandable approach to innovation that expands the opportunities and impact."[11]

While intrapreneurs certainly benefit from a strong internal network, the effort should not end with fellow employees. Relationships can be found in many places. For example, conferences often provide fertile ground for expanding knowledge and fostering relationships. If you're involved in an intrapreneurial project with a strong technology angle, you might attend an industry conference looking for data and platform partners. If you go in ready to engage, you may find a selection of other companies interested in partnering with you. Then you and others are in a position to explore a mutually beneficial relationship that drives new value for you and your customers.

While exploring opportunities, you can engage a wide range of people in corporate innovation and improve many areas of the business, with initiatives large and small. Ultimately, they all can benefit current and new customers while creating value for the organization.

First Principles Approach

For finding and realizing the potential of opportunities, the "first principles approach" has received increasing attention in recent years. Organizational leaders, philosophers, and others have suggested that we should understand the goal(s), confirm what is certain or near certain, and then otherwise discard conventional wisdom and established ways of doing things. It involves breaking down the problem into its most basic parts. This approach works well in multiple situations, especially in transformational innovation efforts as well as serial intrapreneurship.

Teams that I have worked with have also adopted versions of this approach from time to time. It basically involves starting ideation from the ground up. For example, it applied to large-scale efforts when we were imagining multiple generations of the growing new mobile business at The Weather Channel. Also, it worked well with focused, impactful efforts like deploying weather radar images on a new generation of mobile phones or, separately, developing a new iPad news app that wasn't a clone of any other existing product. This approach is powerful and yet also works best with discipline, along with an established system to implement it consistently.

The Evaluation Method Depends on Your Situation

Sometimes we choose to start with a (figurative or literal) blank sheet of paper and work upward toward a goal. Sometimes we have clear indications about the path to pursue in advance, and then can choose to use customer research and deep data mining to shape our plans further. How many times have we heard a debate about one or the other approach being superior? I have, plenty of times. Here's the thing: both have their place and their purposes. Being able to choose which to employ, or a combination, can make the difference between frustrating swings at the plate and home runs—not to mention singles, doubles, and triples along the way. In many cases, what's important is to be in the game, and to step up to the plate. Which approach to deploy depends on the situation, including how transformative your project is expected to be, and the reliability of the insight gleaned from existing resources. In any event, having the capability to use both will provide greater versatility in your innovation over time.

As Marie Quintero-Johnson points out, from time to time you will find situations where someone sees an opportunity that is aligned with the current or future core value proposition of the company, but it has not yet been internalized into the strategy overall. Whatever you may be doing in your team, you're trying to increase the value and relevance of your larger entity, too. You're pushing for strategic and financial gains. That has to be your underlying assumption. The entrepreneur can go for individual glory in a specific field of opportunity; you are a team player from start to finish.

Once you have identified the opportunities, how do you assess and de-risk them? Various methodologies can apply here, and this topic could occupy multiple books and articles on its own. The types of approaches vary from broad strategies to specific tools and narrowly defined processes. However, there are some best practices that our teams have used many times to improve the chances of a positive result. Some of them are both very simple and very powerful.

Do a SWOT Analysis

One example is the SWOT analysis. Do not skip this section.

You may think you know what a SWOT is and that you don't

need it because it's too basic for your innovative idea, so you can skip this part. If that sounds like you, think again.

On the other hand, you may think you need a SWOT, and you already know how to execute a quick and dirty one properly. If so, you may still be leaving opportunity on the table. I know that I underestimated the full utility of this analysis when setting out to craft my early ones as an intrapreneur.

And if SWOT sounds like something you do with a bat and a ball, then you can find more info on what this means for an intrapreneur here. No matter how secure you are in your SWOT knowledge—whether you are pro-SWOT, anti-SWOT, or somewhere in between—read on anyway.

A SWOT analysis (or SWOT matrix) is a widely used strategic technique to understand key factors that affect your business or initiative. The acronym describes a process used to help a person or organization identify the most relevant strengths, weaknesses, opportunities, and threats.

Some people adjust this approach and conduct a TOWS analysis instead of or in addition to the SWOT. This modified approach involves a restructuring of the category order (threats, opportunities, weaknesses, and strengths) typically with similar info, and the inclusion of strategies that derive from pairs of the quadrants. I'm not opposed to this thinking but have found that for intrapreneurs, a SWOT analysis is adequate—and most important—for success. Therefore, for our purposes here, we'll focus on the SWOT itself.

A SWOT analysis plays a very useful role in the preliminary stages of decision-making processes. People use it to evaluate the strategic position of an organization, and it's also a great way to get a wide-angle view of a potential project or venture.

Strengths and weaknesses usually focus on internal factors. Opportunities and threats usually highlight external factors. Earlier in my career, I was more willing to blur the lines on this distinction—after all, many factors are connected and the lines between internal and external get blurry sometimes. Now, however, I try to maintain it diligently to assist with clear thinking and crisp communication. Strengths and weaknesses particularly help to assess what needs to be done in my organization for the idea to be successful. Opportunities and threats typically excel at illuminating the strategic rationale for going after the idea at all.

It's easy enough to follow the grid process of the SWOT procedure. So, let's discuss the reasons to go down this road at all.

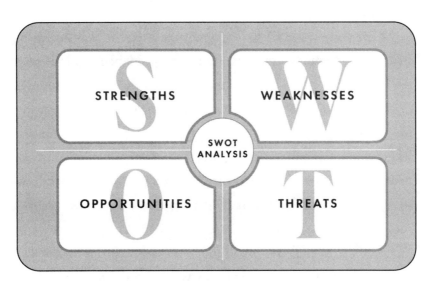

SWOT PROVIDES BRAINSTORMING FUEL

In the early stages of an intrapreneurial project, you want the ideas to flow freely. You need to hear many possibilities, even the wild and crazy ones. You want to leave no idea stone unturned. For that, I recommend brainstorming, and the SWOT framework provides users with a powerful vehicle for that experience. Sure, you can just stand up at the whiteboard and write things down. But the SWOT helps you (and your team) organize and fuel the process.

One reason for effectiveness here is that the SWOT grid is so familiar to many business players. When those four quadrants go up on the board, people around the table know what happens next. It's like a traffic light—everyone understands what the different colors mean. Chances are good, your players know what to do when they see that visual. You'll waste little time explaining the rules of this game.

What's more, the SWOT grid helps to keep the brainstorming from running off the rails. Without any guidance at all, a room full of smart people can converse productively at length focused on one single area of the intrapreneurial idea, let's say, strengths, for example. Now, that's fun—sitting around, throwing out reasons the idea is terrific and going to make this business really take off. The energy in the room during a strengths-focused session will often be high, but it won't get you close enough to a successful intrapreneurial project alone. Instead, the brainstorming needs to hit all the quadrants. And you, as the leader, can keep the brainstorming on track by watching the sections fill up.

Imagine guiding the discussion; once you develop the strengths quadrant, you're ready to use your visual to move the brainstorming in a new direction: "Let's look at weaknesses." "Now let's spend the next thirty minutes solely on opportunities." "And let's round it out with threats." The SWOT grid gives you the authority to move the brainstorming energy where it needs to go, and then you'll have a multifaceted view of some of the driving considerations for your growth concept.

SWOT PROVIDES DISCIPLINE

In the early stages of any innovation, a lot of options will fly around the room, the virtual meeting, or the email thread. Everyone will want to toss in their latest bright idea.

The SWOT process is a discipline in and of itself. It provides a literal framework to gather ideas and sort them into buckets. It can help to minimize the risk of having a disproportionate perspective on certain angles of the business. Sometimes, you'll have a group that is very energetic but doesn't understand the challenges adequately. Sometimes, and especially in a business that faces major headwinds, you can fill up the weaknesses and threats to the extent that they overshadow the very real strengths. Thoughtful balance greatly benefits the intrapreneur who wants to assess the situation accurately.

In the early phases of the SWOT process, I encourage you to generate dozens of ideas for consideration in each part of the grid. You might have quadrants with twenty or thirty items in each. And that's fine. This is the way you bring focus and clarity to the still-forming ideas. You may find overlap. You may find bullets that can be combined. But having a way to bring all the ideas into the discussion in a coherent, organized fashion is valuable.

Ultimately, you will edit this list down. I find the most successful final SWOT summaries generally have about five bullets (and sometimes fewer) per quadrant. But those other ideas and observations are not wasted. You may remove them from the grid for now but save them for potential reference at a later date. Think of this process as building a compressed accordion. You can expand and contract it as the need arises.

SWOT MAKES A FOUNDATIONAL SLIDE

Let's have a moment of real talk: companies can make it very hard to bring forth new, innovative ideas. You can have a hundred conversations—meetings, one-on-ones, email threads—and still find you're treading water.

SWOT gives you a foundational slide, a reference point from which many other topics flow. And a foundational slide can make a huge difference. By the way, if you work in an environment that minimizes slide use, then you can include the same info together in narrative form for similar effect.

If accurate and carefully constructed, then the SWOT enables your idea, on one slide, to emerge as a strategic initiative with clarity and layers of insight. A SWOT slide, on one page, illustrates the value creation potential of the idea as well as the needs and concerns related to the proposal. I've never found a better visual as a grounding mechanism for such a wide range of businesses.

And that's important because, let's face it, so much of corporate communication today lives by slideware. A great slide illustrates your idea and engages your audience in the time it takes to double click. It delivers your idea in an easy-to-remember format. Everyone who sees it knows what you're trying to do and how they can help.

Consider the alternative: with no SWOT slide, you can spend hours, even days, trying to explain the opportunity to everyone. All that work when a slide will do the trick. Yes, a slide is worth a thousand words. No—a hundred thousand or more.

Then, once you've created a SWOT slide, your idea can gain traction. The slide then flies around an enterprise much faster than you can set up meetings. It becomes your messenger to the decision-makers.

For example, Pascal Racheneur, a digital product and technology leader with expertise in media and financial technology, recalls a time when this approach crystallized some business-changing insights. He says, "A SWOT analysis reinforced that The Weather Channel had an opportunity to leverage its strength in data and technology to launch new products and services for consumers outside the US. This led to the development of a business plan for and launch of a revived international division focusing on desktop and mobile offerings."[12]

Many decision-makers find value in the clarity of a SWOT. Finance teams in particular typically love the simplicity of a well-constructed one. They may agree or disagree, but the SWOT slide gives them something to hold on to. It cuts through unnecessary discussion and provides an on-ramp to more data points by grounding the financial analysis. It enables the related data on return on investment (ROI) to grab their attention and hold it. Without these combined pieces of information, your slide can become just another trial balloon someone is floating—not yet worthy of attention.

SWOT = Distilled Insight

SWOT = Simplicity

SWOT = Context for More Data

For some audiences, that's all they want to know.

A final word on SWOT: don't send your first SWOT diagram out into the enterprise. Instead, work on it a bit, and then some more. Put it through the washing machine a few times. Your first iteration, even if it came out of a full-day off-site in which everyone focused solely on this project, can probably be improved. Three iterations is a good rule of thumb as a minimum. Once you hit send, that image is out there and it's impossible to put the genie back in the bottle. You may send out updates, but that first one will often be hanging around—and has made a first impression. Save yourself the trouble and edit before you hit send.

We've spent a good bit of time on this topic. Here's why: the SWOT analysis is really valuable, but it isn't actually about the slide. Not even close. It's not solely about the individual insights on it, or the process to generate new business opportunities that will benefit large numbers of people. When this exercise is done well, it's actually practicing age-old and broadly applicable wisdom related to generating accurate, meaningful, and actionable self-understanding. In fact, "Know Thyself" was carved in stone on the entrance to Apollo's temple at Delphi in Greece. Lao Tzu observed that "Knowing others is wisdom, knowing yourself is Enlightenment." While our focus at this point is more about the organization than the individual, that kind of understanding is what we're looking for. So while we dedicate ourselves to building knowledge through situation assessment, let's remember to go beyond the slides and the team exercises, no matter how valuable. Let's make sure to recognize that we can serve our organization, our customers, and ourselves much better with professional insights on our situation that come through a process like this one. This hard work helps us assess the current business situation and opportunities more accurately, and in turn leads directly to expanded opportunities to attain our full potential.

Understand Your Parent Company's Culture and Priorities

Know your mothership.

I present this as the next item on our list but do not consider it solely in a linear fashion. It's something you should be working on all the time. Even while thinking about what might work in the marketplace, every intrapreneur should also be scanning the internal enterprise for indications about the current biggest needs, stated priorities, and level of risk tolerance for new ventures. This awareness is fundamental to understanding which initiatives will work and which ones will never get off the ground, no matter how innovative and well-presented.

Remember that your environment differs from that of an entrepreneur. You work inside the corporate confines. In Chapter 1 we established that you need a core understanding of the overall corporate priorities. Intrapreneurial opportunities should align with these goals. When you know the company's strategy and priorities, you can also understand more about where its biggest needs lie.

So, what are the strengths and weaknesses of your broader organization—beyond the intrapreneurial venture that you're focused on and beyond the scope of your initiative's SWOT analysis? Some of them you may already know. Others you'll have to go looking for.

It's easy enough to find information on your company's strengths. Many people internally will talk about them freely. Various documents will trumpet them—in places like internal presentations, quarterly reports, annual reports, press releases, and official corporate social media.

That's all useful information.

To get to the weaknesses, you can look for internal resources as well as outside critiques such as analyst reports and media coverage.

But to make sure you have the most comprehensive information on internal weaknesses, talk with coworkers.

In any company I've been part of, current team members have a wealth of knowledge about where the weaknesses are found. It sometimes takes some intrapreneurial moxie to address these issues. Some are inherent and will not change; others present opportunities to innovate. Understand the difference, and you will have valuable perspective on choosing where to focus your efforts.

Another area to understand is your company's regulatory environment. You can have the best, most innovative idea in the world, but if it flies in the face of your firm's regulatory requirements, it will rarely happen. In addition to knowing the regulatory rules, consider also the related current and future potential challenges. What are the rules issues that are most troublesome? Most difficult to wrangle? Can your project address a regulatory pain point? In particular, it's worth paying close attention to data privacy and protection. When you know what your company deals with every day, you can tailor your project to meet that challenge.

Ultimately, when you steep yourself in the strengths, weaknesses, and priorities of the broader organization, you will better align yourself with the corporate vision. You can read a mission statement a thousand times. But if you really want to internalize what a company needs, immerse yourself in what it does well, and where it is vulnerable. No matter what the mission statement may say, capitalizing on strengths and shoring up weaknesses is core to the mission of any successful enterprise.

Understanding your enterprise is also where you will learn what behaviors you will need as a leader to make intrapreneurship happen. If you hope to lead an intrapreneurial team, you'll need to know when and how team members can be deployed. Who can you ask to help you? Who can you expect to support (or block) you? How can you give employees broad discretion to innovate within the confines of the enterprise? If you know a lot about your firm's dynamics, you can make strategic internal decisions that are operationally sound and also dovetail with the varying needs of the larger organization.

Test Your Assumptions

Your final step in the opportunity scanning process: put your newly minted assumptions to the test. There are several options you can pursue (and again, intrapreneurs often have more options than entrepreneurs).

One is to conduct empirical research that is specific to your intrapreneurial initiative. This means doing real testing with real customers, partners, and services. This may be something you can do in-house, or it may be a project you conduct jointly with an outside firm. Often, empirical research plays a critical role at an early stage. An entrepreneur can sometimes fly on a hunch. A larger enterprise generally requires numbers to move forward at scale. When it's time to test the assumptions, it's often also time to engage professionals to run the numbers. You don't always need a budget for this, but you can benefit from expert insights to have the highest probability of success.

Ways to gather info include hands-on customer testing with prototype products, question-based surveys, and diagnostic testing with technical tools to measure things like server response time. You may find there's enough interest internally to set up your own testing processes. We certainly did this more than once at The Weather Channel. We ran our programs on a series of software platforms to test performance. In the marketplace, we tested different types of advertising (including ads on parking shuttle buses at major airports). We also took our mobile products on road shows to gauge customer responses.

In situations like these, there is no substitute for meeting directly with current and potential clients to hear comments and assess levels of interest. Derek Van Nostran tells this story from his long-ago ad agency days: "My favorite story is when we went and got a worldwide hotel chain's entire digital marketing budget before they had digital marketing. They had never used an agency for digital marketing before. We had never placed a digital ad before. But we convinced them to invest several million dollars of digital marketing with us."[13] Often, when you venture out on the road and get in front of the customer, new possibilities emerge that benefit all parties.

Another option is to use research that is not specific to your intrapreneurial initiative but does provide contextual information.

Some of this may be more general about things like market size, and some of it may be specific to your company in ways that you can apply to understand your initiative better. When practical, use this information both before you launch your empirical research and along the way to calibrate it better.

Regardless of the approach you choose, testing and searching for empirical data does not suggest you lack confidence in your idea. In fact, some of the most respected voices in innovation insist on it. Look at the work of Jim Collins, author of books such as *Built to Last*, *Good to Great*, and *Great by Choice*. He has written extensively on the efforts of industry-leading companies as they seek innovations that will expand and enhance their success. Collins says that testing should be part of the path to greatness. Generating empirical data early on is a powerful way to elevate your ability to make sound decisions as an intrapreneur. Once you have more information on what works well, you can then expand your level of investment while simultaneously decreasing risk.

Testing assumptions can be time-consuming, but it will save backtracking and revision later on. It will also provide you with supporting reference material should you encounter opposition to your idea early in the building process.

You may have the seed of an idea in mind, but before starting an intrapreneurial project, take the time to examine the full landscape. The key is to identify ways to build a standalone business that will be strategically aligned with and accretive to the core business. By calibrating the opportunities in advance, you better pave the way for success with a larger investment. Armed with information, support, and an understanding of the marketplace, you're ready to dive into the work of getting your idea off the ground.

Chapter Summary

In this chapter, we walk through the steps an intrapreneur should follow to evaluate growth options and make sound decisions among them.

- Understand your organization's strategy thoroughly.

- Shape your intrapreneurial efforts to support and amplify the overall strategy.

- Assess the external marketplace for opportunities, with a particular focus on known and potential customer needs.

- Build capabilities to evaluate ideas, both relying on your treasure trove of preexisting data and also "blank sheet of paper" transformational thinking. Each has its place.

- Create a concise SWOT analysis to understand and communicate the current landscape of your proposed initiative.

- Assess the practicality of advancing your idea internally, using knowledge of the broader organization, including risk tolerance and timing.

CHAPTER 3

CRAFT THE STRATEGY

One day in February 2011, I felt a surge of adrenaline while stepping onto the stage at an event in Mountain View, California. Other CNN team members and I had traveled there to announce the launch of the new CNN app for Android tablets to accompany the rollout of "Honeycomb," the third version of Google's Android operating system. After months of planning and weeks of intense development work, we were ready to unveil the new product.

The room buzzed with the chatter of people from many different areas—media, entertainment, technology. What's more, the event was covered by the press worldwide. Lila King, our head of citizen journalism service iReport, joined me on stage for the announcement and we tag-teamed with Google team members and other speakers at this milestone for the platform and the evolution of tablets. The project marked a major step forward for CNN, which had been investing aggressively to grow in the mobile space.

It marked a victory, too, for our team, which had worked within the walls of a big media company to carve out this unique product, building on our overall business strategy that included a commitment to innovative apps on major platforms worldwide.

But the journey to Mountain View wasn't easy. What got us on the stage that day was intrapreneurial strategy combined with patience and hard work.

In this chapter, we look closely at the process of crafting a strategy for an intrapreneurial venture. To have the highest chances of success, ensure you have a stated strategic approach as you set out on your intrapreneurial journey. Generally, you will have a limited number of opportunities to demonstrate success of a new concept. In some cases, you may even have only one or two big chances before other corporate leaders pull the plug and tell you to quit dreaming up crazy new stuff and get back to work.

Because of these limitations, you should invest time and energy into crafting a strategy for the venture early on—even if you or others feel impatient just to get going.

Let's walk through the steps of a smart intrapreneurial strategy.

Begin with the End in Mind

Envision an idea that is timeless. Stephen Covey emphasized this powerful concept in his famous *7 Habits of Highly Effective*

People. It's so important that "Begin with the end in mind" is Covey's Habit No. 2 (Right after "Be Proactive").[1] Covey asked individuals to use this concept to plan out their most effective personal strategies. We use it here for an intrapreneurial project.

When you begin with the end in mind, you're envisioning the ultimate goal of your initiative. You consider why your efforts matter, think through options, decide on the preferred outcome, and commit it to a summary—ideally a concise sentence or phrase. When you do this, write it down. Put your *end* on paper and give it concrete manifestation. This helps you (and others who hear about your project) stay on track. A commitment to defining and sharing your destination is an early step in creating a true road map to success.

Here's an example of that in action. I arrived at CNN in the middle of 2009. While the company had been leading in digital services for years, mobile-optimized capabilities and products were still in their early stages of development. The company had understandably focused on other areas and had put limited intentionality around this one. A new level of mobile excellence was waiting in the wings of the business, and several forward-looking leaders identified it as an area ripe for intrapreneurial growth. But to do that, we had to have a strategy. And a strategy benefits from a definition of the time frame involved, too.

After some careful review, including consideration of options to address a wide range of needs, our team identified two primary and well-understood indicators of success: monthly unique users and revenue. We then agreed upon aggressive, primary, overarching goals for these two metrics in 2012, three years into the future. We set out to reach millions of monthly users and generate millions of dollars in revenue in that time frame. With these two simple shared objectives in mind, we organized our efforts and then accomplished some amazing things in the following years.

We presented an audacious outlook at the start, to be sure. By having an end in mind, we were consistently underscoring our strategic plan: be more relevant to users, thereby growing total usage, and as a result, increasing revenue in a way that collectively complemented our other platforms. This last point is highly important—it was not about mobile in a vacuum; it was about mobile as a platform to strengthen the company's overall strategy.

These plans were simple and easy to understand. And they did not bog down in details—yet. If, at that point in the process, we only went around giving extensive talks on the business's wide range of needs in excruciating detail, eyes would glaze over. It would be too in the weeds for the early strategy creation. People wanted to know that we had a vision, a destination.

While taking early steps, you should be able to communicate where those steps will lead your company over a longer time. You need to show that you have the end in mind. If you can't articulate end goals, you risk never getting out of the starting gate. When you share the primary goals consistently (often with the related rationale on why they matter), you have a core building block for success.

This mandate is not unique to intrapreneurs. Most business leaders who want strong support must do this. But the concept weighs particularly heavy on the intrapreneur. To get started, you'll have to convince a lot of people that you know what you're doing. You'll need buy-in. At CNN, in order to achieve our full potential, we needed support from over one hundred people who had lots of other things to think about at the time (some worked not just at CNN but also at our parent company Turner Broadcasting). We needed to convey that we were beginning with the end in mind—and that destination was going to be both meaningful and memorable.

Vision, Goals, and Values

That first effort will lead you into the broader strategy process. A superior intrapreneurial strategy needs a coherent and aligned combination of vision, goals, and values.

The *end* that we just covered is a good example of a goal. Now, let's talk about vision.

Your overall goal with specific milestones and metrics, while exciting and compelling, does not constitute a vision. A vision (also called a "mission statement" by some companies) is a bigger concept with a broader root structure and fewer details. While a goal is specific, even time-stamped, a vision should generally be evergreen. For example, LinkedIn's vision is, "Create economic opportunity for every member of the global workforce."[2] For IKEA, the vision is "To create a better everyday life for the many people."[3] With our CNN mobile business, we wanted to engage people worldwide on mobile platforms in the service of our overarching company vision too.

As with many similar companies, mobile became a critical part of the overall company strategy. That was especially true for a news organization that had grown over time primarily based on its cable TV offerings and was developing a fast-growing, broader digital business. Our team was articulating a big, audacious vision. It wasn't the same as our *quantitative goals*, which were now enshrined in our working strategy. Our goals included a date. Our goals included a number. Two numbers, actually. Our goals were grounded in specifics, albeit aspirational ones. By contrast, our vision soared above the details and gave us an evergreen statement we could use during that time frame (through 2012) and beyond. We committed to getting the support and buy-in needed to fulfill our vision and achieve our goals.

One note: Sometimes people get into a debate about vision and mission. In general, I see a "vision" as an evergreen aspirational statement typically not defined by a specific time frame. It often applies for as long as the organization exists. If there are changes, they are usually few and far between. On the other hand, I have generally viewed a "mission" as a broad and valuable statement that tends to be quantifiable and time-defined. Some people see these terms as synonyms. On more than one occasion, I've participated in discussions about which word to use for which purpose. In any event, regardless of the words you use, I would advise always having both 1) a broad, evergreen, and aspirational statement that fits the definition of a vision here, and 2) a longer-term transformational goal that is quantifiable and meaningful to the organization—whether it goes by the term "mission" or "three-year goal" or any other label. Pick your terms, and then make sure that you have the substance.

Next, we move on to articulating our values.

Too many intrapreneurs skip this step. A group of corporate employees around a conference table may not see the need. After all, this is not a gathering of a few founders in a garage trying to come up with a standalone company. As employees of an enterprise, you've likely been through values discussions during onboarding, at off-sites, and in any number of training sessions. Why talk about values now?

I take this exercise very seriously. You can gain a lot from the values of the mothership as an intrapreneur, especially if they have been thoughtfully developed. Of course, as employees, you also need to live and honor them. At the same time, an intrapreneurial venture benefits from a set of shared values that are defined by team members attached to the venture. We then apply values as part of the strategy to ensure everyone else on the team is also on the same page over time.

The intrapreneur should not do this exercise alone; this is a job for the team. At the end of the day, the team will have to live these values.

Over time, I've repeatedly developed values statements from scratch with my own teams for different ventures, while retaining awareness of the ones expressed by the parent organization. I know many others have done this as well. In general, I prefer to generate values based around single words. Single words stick. They may be followed by an explanatory sentence. But the word itself should do most of the heavy lifting. You should be able to hear it, say it, and live it without a lot of additional information.

As an example, I prefer to include the word *integrity* in any values exercise of this sort. I place it at or near the top. It sets the tone early and makes everyone think about what's most important. It sends a very powerful signal about expectations and attracts people who share it and live it viscerally. While most people that I've worked with over time also see this value as fundamental, that's not universally true. And when we find a gap in behavior versus this expectation, we can then address it.

Integrity brings people together and builds trust. It prevents issues that can harm a business, undermine service to customers, and divide a team. If you're on this team, we expect that it's a high-ranking value for you, one you live by always as a guidance mechanism for whatever comes next. When we list integrity prominently, it acts as a primary defining characteristic not just for individuals, but also for the team overall.

What are some other terms that provide the most important ongoing reminders? *Respect* emerges as a common and powerful one. So does *curiosity*. Others include *creativity, effort, action-orientation, excellence, risk-taking,* and *having fun along the way.* You will have the opportunity to craft the list that works for you, your project, and your team. The process of generating your team's values will help you to move toward your goals with confidence and mutual trust.

Articulate Your Core Business Rationale

With your core ideas and concepts in place, create connection to the larger enterprise as your next strategic step.

You're not an entrepreneur, you're an intrapreneur, and in this context your idea requires relevance to its value to the company. Display that connection in this section of your strategy.

Your goal at this stage is to build a bridge between the opportunity you see in the marketplace and what the company is hoping to achieve on a broader scale. This pushes you to draft a plan highlighting a space in the business world that you think is worth focusing on. You do this by showing your idea has value to the broader enterprise. It may be a way to serve existing customers better, bring new customers into the fold, save money, or even expand the leadership position of the overall enterprise. Your reasoning will be your own. But this bridge between corporate strategy and your idea should be developed now and woven into the fabric of your initiative's strategy.

The best idea in the world will fall flat if you cannot explain and advocate for this connection. Intrapreneurs take initiative, but they can't reinvent their company from the ground up. You must be able to articulate the core business rationale for your venture—not just for your idea, but also for your company's support of it. This bridge represents a critical aspect of your strategy.

Although typically involving focus, teamwork, and creativity, the process of developing a strategy does not need to be intimidating. Bahns Stanley, longtime investor and former EVP of strategy and development at The Weather Channel, makes this observation:

Many people think strategy is complicated and daunting. I think you really need to answer just a few questions, and that can yield a strategy. You can always start with an internal/external SWOT analysis to evaluate where you stand, but SWOT is no substitute for the following:

1. What are the objectives? They could be financial—sales growth, profit, cash flow, etc. They could be operational—market share/leadership, launching products, entering new territories.

2. What resources do we need that we don't have today to achieve those objectives? The answers could include things like capital, workforce talent, manufacturing capacity, relationships with suppliers/distributors/customers, etc.

3. How do we get the necessary resources? Can we build or hire? Do we need to acquire or partner with a company/competitor to fill in the gaps we have? What are our financial requirements, and how can we secure budget for them?

If we can't get the resources to achieve the objectives, then we don't have a realistic strategy. In that case, start over and rethink your objectives.[4]

He goes on to say that we often think of strategy for a period of about three to five years, and beyond that in certain long-cycle situations. But there can sometimes be a need to think very short-term. So while developing a strategy, an intrapreneur should generally ground thinking in longer timeframes and also be willing to adjust the time horizon as needed to match the current business requirements.

At this juncture, as you develop the strategy, overemphasize the business plan. The business plan is important for most types of innovative ventures. That said, it's easy to underestimate its importance in a large company. Many intrapreneurs are doers. They have a vision, and they want to get going. They are impatient. And yet this is another place where moving too fast can cost time, credibility, and resources. Take the time to really think through your plan . . . and get buy-in along the way.

Distinguished media leader and former global CNN chief marketing officer Scot Safon says the failure to envision this bridge is often an intrapreneur's downfall. "When I've seen frustrated intrapreneurs, it's usually because they know in their heart it's a great idea, but they haven't really thought it through," he says. "You're asking the company to make an investment. The investment needs to have a return. That return doesn't necessarily have to be revenue, but it has to be something to build the business and build the relationship with the customer."[5] This is the moment to articulate that rationale.

Decker Anstrom, a media executive who served as president and CEO of the National Cable Television Association (NCTA), president of The Weather Channel (TWC), and president of its parent company Landmark Communications, highlighted how a major brand emerged from within another company as a prototypical example of intrapreneurship. He and others repeatedly emphasized to me how The Weather Channel grew in a succession of bold steps while under multiple generations of Batten family ownership. You might be thinking about weather.com emerging from TWC, but Decker actually shined a light into an earlier, foundational stage of development.

The Weather Channel gained its footing within the media company Landmark Communications in the early 1980s. Multiple visionary leaders supported it, including Frank Batten Sr., John "Dubby" Wynne, and John Coleman. In reference to the transformational power of intrapreneurship, Decker noted that "The Weather Channel is a perfect example of that. The teams at Landmark and The Weather Channel really thought it was going to work. They did their homework and then implemented a thoughtful action plan. And Landmark made a major commitment. They lost a lot of money for an extended time. But they had a clear eye about what the assumptions were that would lead to success or not."[6] By articulating the core value of the idea, the early leaders of TWC were able to sustain support even as major financial challenges occurred before the business could fully gain its upward momentum. The well-articulated rationale gave everyone a point on the horizon to focus on. And the decision-makers within the parent business had the foresight and guts to stick with it.

Remember at this stage that you're an intrapreneur and not an entrepreneur. Early on, value-adding innovation and revenue are more important than some other factors, and typically much more important than near-term profitability. Unlike many ventures where cash is truly king, for intrapreneurial ventures this usually is not the primary challenge at all, at least not at an enterprise level. Yes, you still need cash to invest in the business, and to drive profitability over time. However, successful large businesses typically have lots of cash. Some have cash flowing like a fire hydrant. What they need are good ideas and promising growth businesses. If you can drive acceptable revenue growth at a short-term loss with a reasonable expectation of profitable growth over time, you have a great opportunity in front of you. This is unlike many entrepreneurial situations, where cash availability stops some businesses that would have more resources and a longer runway in a larger organization. It also means that intrapreneurs can spend more time on building the business and less on the next round of fundraising (offset, of course, by continuing communication with corporate teammates!).

Share Business Unit Goals

This step takes the goals you've generated and makes them more specific and actionable. At this stage, we try to boil the relevant ones down into the most compact statements possible and get them onto a single page in very large font—and it's usually on a presentation slide. Then, I make sure this slide appears as the first substantive content in just about every presentation we give going forward.

It doesn't matter if that's not the primary topic of the discussion. I may be getting up to talk about the technology of our project or the financing or the overall marketplace. Doesn't matter. This summary of goals clicks in at Slide 2—just after the cover slide. It reminds everyone I present to that this team has established goals and we're sticking to them. It's a reminder that we're a serious concern and that we have a vision of the path to achieving high potential that will be meaningful to the broader organization.

This slide provides other stakeholders with a visual that says we have a strategy, and we are executing it.

This one little slide can help you stay on track, even when you are still in the early, formative stages of your project. You may be onto something big—however, to sustain support internally, it's still essential to help others understand how your project connects to the company's broader needs. By establishing your goals (and by displaying them often), you remind everyone around you that you're not just going through the motions. You are a force, small but mighty.

Further, the routine presentation of goals (preferably paired with values on a following slide) helps build corporate support. Whatever wild, imaginative thing you are working on, the language of goals and values will become familiar to your corporate teammates. As you move forward, they'll recognize it and it reminds them: no, we are not a bunch of renegades operating without regard to the needs of the broader company; we are all on the same team, part of the same family.

Creating that sense of belonging is critical. If I've learned anything in my years in corporations, it's that there is such a thing as a "corporate immune system," and when it senses an intruder, it throws up its defenses. When you express familiar points such as goals and values, these reference points help the company embrace you as one of its own.

This kind of language will help others support you. If you bring your plan to your boss and your boss's boss and get approval to proceed, sooner or later, those individuals may be called upon to explain what you and your team are actually up to. At that point, those people will need a short but compelling answer. The audience may want to hear more from you or from others. But at that moment, the needed information comes from Slide 2.

The team is committed to X. Its specific goals are Y and Z. It will benefit the broader organization in ABC ways.

Here's a rough general view of how that might have appeared on my slide, back in 2009.

The team is committed to building a world-class mobile business. Its goals are X million customers and $Y million in revenue over a 3-year time frame. We're committed to making mobile a primary way that CNN engages with customers, while complementing our other CNN platforms.

End of slide.

This type of definitive statement calms a lot of corporate nerves. Trust me; as an intrapreneur, you need as much support as you can muster.

Here's my list of "must-have" slides for the intrapreneur:

1. Cover page with your initiative's name and the parent company logo on it

2. Vision and goals

3. Values

4. SWOT analysis

5. Proposed strategy

6. Market assessment (research-based)

7. Target customers

8. Product summary

9. Technology requirements

10. Financial analysis

11. Recommendation for resource allocation (team, financial, time, research, etc.)

12. Next steps

You will not use all of these slides for every purpose. But you should have all of them available to include and adapt as core elements of communication for multiple audiences.

Identify Resources Required

Naturally, the project you pursue will demand resources. The questions now emerge: what, how much, and how can you best ask for and receive what you need?

To do this, I suggest you reverse the title of this section. Start with the word *required*. What does your project actually need? This is a place where your needs and those of an entrepreneur are very similar. To answer the question, you can move into the oft used minimum viable product (MVP) analysis made famous by Eric Ries in his book *The Lean Startup*.[7] You will surely have a vision for what would be ideal. Perhaps you even have clarity on what you deem necessary. But look at that wish list hard and be honest: what's your minimum? You may not be able to get the resources to create the best and most spectacular version of your project, but you need enough to ensure you can get something out the door. That baseline understanding can act as your catalyst for additional support.

What do you need for your MVP? Keep in mind that it's always much more than just money. Certainly, financial resources are part of the equation, but the bigger and far more difficult area to excel in for many is bringing the right people on board. In my experience, it's often harder to get approval for headcount (corporate speak for other people who will focus on your project, especially if they do this full-time) than it is to get approval for dollars. The truth is that dollars are less complicated to allocate. Any company leader knows that if you spend money on something one year and it does well, you generally spend again (and likely invest even more). If it doesn't go well, then next year you can adjust accordingly.

When applying this type of thinking to an evaluation of team roles required for success, you face other important questions as well. This process involves not just resource allocation questions, but also other ethical ones. How do we best take care of people? If you hire a group of new team members one year and the project they work on goes well, wonderful. You hire them, train them, and maybe even hire more. But if it does not . . . backing off an investment in people is a lot more painful than backing off an investment in dollars. For this big reason, getting approval for hiring in an intrapreneurial project may be one of the most difficult hurdles to clear.

What's more, you'll need to consider other non-monetary needs as well. Chances are that you'll need access to internal information such as market research or competitive intelligence. You may need additional training. You may need access to customers—and that's sometimes very sensitive. Think of it this way: suppose your intrapreneurial idea involves reaching out to customers who already buy advertising on your platform. You want to talk with them, but you may find the client account managers standing firmly in your way. Not all will be comfortable letting you have direct communication with their customers.

These are all resources that are harder than plain old dollars to secure. But you'll still need them.

Then we come to another primary resource most everyone in an intrapreneurial role today will need: technology capabilities and capacity. Information technology (IT) resources—software engineers, architects, data scientists, operations team members, and technical project managers, for example—are the technical experts who are often critical to innovative ideas. And they are therefore often among the busiest people in the firm. Getting the time and attention from your technology experts may at times be the hardest resource to secure of all.

And I would be remiss if I didn't mention one more resource: time. Your best plans will stall if you can't get the allocation of time for yourself and for your team. Understanding the time demands and what your team can contribute represents a key resource to consider early on.

Strategy Stages

Your first cracks at strategy will often be conceptual. You'll be working to create broader concepts such as vision, mission, and overall strategic priorities. You'll be thinking big and broadly. But that's a stage and in this push to create a clarified strategy for your project, some concrete elements will need to emerge further.

When that wraps up, it's time to get down to the how-to of this project. That means turning your efforts from conceptual thinking to applied business strategy. Intrapreneurship is practical. And as a practical discipline, at least some of your strategy needs to be connected to the reality of what the business actually needs. Not just broader observations such as "mobile will be big someday." Even if that's true, what does it mean? Will people use apps or mobile web? What technology infrastructure will or will not be available, and on what timeline? Where do you have partners that will want to work with you actively in the near future? Where do you expect to see slow rolling? Where can you get proof-of-concept revenue earlier, or will it come later? All of these things and more contribute to a consolidated, applied business strategy that you can really activate.

My arrival at CNN provides a case in point. From day one, we were in the thick of a very intense building period. The media company enjoyed a global brand and company leadership had high ambitions for mobile. The company was already developing its first iPhone app, actively exploring new developer partnerships, and expanding relationships with some of the biggest names in Silicon Valley. It was a time of considerable turbulence and urgency that we all felt keenly.

So, we took action and continued to focus on the current handful of strategically central projects. We were all in agreement on this.

Also, we proposed accelerating even more and immediately allocating some major additional investment to this promising mobile growth business. Given the many needs related to our near-term opportunities, I thought our EVP might be willing to provide a quick approval for more resources. Instead, she applied the insights gained from similar experiences in the past. In a way that was both supportive and clear, she shared that while we continued to focus on current commitments, we weren't going to be hiring and investing more than needed for current operations and plans yet—until we outlined the mobile business strategy. In writing. And in detail.

We had to prioritize and multitask. We would have to toggle between immediate operating priorities and the business strategy. Yes, it was very important to make some choices about operational areas. Also, we needed the business strategy documented before they would make additional investments.

We were prioritizing and focusing rigorously. We had to build and launch the iPhone app, run the existing business including mobile web and video, and develop the strategy at the same time, without incremental hiring. Otherwise, no new initiatives, no new Android app, and no replacement yet for our mobile web platform. We decided to focus in particular on building the iPhone app while developing the strategy in the background. The EVP offered to increase support for our very skilled ad sales team's efforts while our product and technology teams focused on making sure the app worked properly.

We could not ignore the fact that the iPhone app prototype we had needed more work. The app needed some user interface (UI) changes and wasn't stable enough yet. In addition to meeting our own high standards, we needed to ensure a positive experience for a premium auto brand that had sponsored the app launch. With focused dedication, our cross-functional team addressed an extraordinary number of individual needs in a short time, and we made great progress toward our project goals.

We then completed the first CNN iPhone app and launched it in September of 2009, after what seemed like a nonstop whirlwind of development and testing.

With the app in place, we shifted more focus to the strategy, while still working to address some app needs. Then, we presented the business strategy to senior executives and secured buy-in for the approach involving further investment and growth. With that support, we still needed to hire team members, build infrastructure, engage with design, and prove that we could generate revenue including through new ad technologies.

We did this even though we also badly wanted to move other projects forward too, including development of an Android app. But we did not have the resources to handle them at that time, and so we maintained relationships and repeated the refrain: we plan to build it, but we need to have the resources to do it right. Though this approach involved compromise, it turned out to be the best move in an imperfect situation, given our resources and needs to build the infrastructure to serve our customers. After we had taken care of several other critical needs, we later turned our attention and resources to the Android app.

And when this work was done, I found myself on that stage in Mountain View— sharing more about our app for Android, demonstrating its capabilities, and underscoring our commitment to presence on mobile devices around the world.

Thanks to a succession of strategic choices, our vision came true.

Now, making the case for support of a new venture differs from actual approval. And to be sure, your skills in developing a proposal count for a lot. At the same time, you want to be in an organization that values growth and will back up that perspective with a willingness to invest in the future. This type of organization will place high priority on investments in new growth initiatives, even as it balances them with support of more established lines of business. While connecting its decisions to overall strategy, these forward-looking organizations will adapt investment criteria to the needs of growth businesses specifically, and not just use the same broad-brush factors for all groups. The willingness to do this comes from the top.

As Decker Anstrom notes on organizational alignment with new ventures, "Part of that signaling comes from the CEO. And maybe it's part of what the intrapreneur helps the CEO understand, is that a spreadsheet can't provide the answer to that. This is what business knowledge and experience tells you about where are the opportunities for the company. Particularly if you're in a company where there is slowing growth in maturing businesses, the safe bet again is to put it in the legacy business. But where's the overall company going to be in three, five, ten years? It's not a spreadsheet. It helps you, right? In the end, the experience and people around you and your decision will have to have a contribution."[8]

In terms of securing support for investment in growth ventures, consumer products and health services innovator Ashlee Adams observes that "it has to do with senior leadership and a good innovation culture. It is top-down. There is an element of if you see from senior leadership that they are supporting risk-taking, that transforms the culture. The people who are enacting this may be at a lower level, not your C-level."[9]

And yet, the C-level support will be evident. Ashlee recalled hosting a mini-conference for one hundred senior leaders, start-ups, and investors for a large multinational. The CEO not only spoke at the gathering but also attended throughout.

That's the kind of "walking the talk" that you want to see

in a company that will drive innovation. By combining your thoughtfully presented strategy, innovative ideas, and practical action to build, you can create some magic—not to mention great value for your organization.

Chapter Summary

In this chapter, we dive into the heart of intrapreneurial strategy and explore how to translate ideas and observations into a plan, setting the stage for sustained successful delivery over time.

- Establish your core statements early, including vision, goals, and values.

- Articulate your business rationale to support the core statements.

- Identify required resources, understanding which ones are truly needed for an MVP.

- Build a summary strategy and planning document in about a dozen slides (or the equivalent) to guide discussions with different audiences.

- Make the hard decisions about prioritization before starting.

- Prepare for action, ambiguity, and changes on the path to launch, while maintaining strategic clarity.

PART II

MAKE IT
HAPPEN

I n this section, we move from planning to action. Even as your project gets under-way, ensure that you understand the stages of rollout and the order of operations, while retaining flexibility to adjust as needed. What you do—and when you do it—will impact your project, your team, and your company.

CHAPTER 4

BUILD AND SUSTAIN
THE TEAM

The time has come to build your intrapreneurial team.

Up to this point, you may have been working mostly solo. Or if you already have a team around you, it's often a small one made up of flexible individuals who can play multiple roles. This makes perfect sense. In its early days, a project frequently doesn't have the focus or the resources to hire specialists, so the early team is often the multitasking team.

In many ways, this tracks the experience of the entrepreneur. The entrepreneurial effort will often begin with one or two individuals with a great idea. The early team will be their close associates—maybe coworkers, industry colleagues, classmates, or family members. This group will forge ahead in the first days, doing everything from defining product specs to writing code to taking out the trash. Sooner or later though, if the idea is good enough, this early team must grow up and allocate more respon-sibilities among more team members.

The same applies to intrapreneurs. The team must grow up and grow out. You'll need to build and sustain a team. However, the process of building that team as an intrapreneur will differ in important ways.

In this chapter, we go through the key steps of intrapreneur-ial team building. We focus intently on the "who" and "how" of that process. And we also take a careful look at an element that is often forgotten: how to sustain a team.

Identifying Structure and Talent

You've already worked to identify the opportunity and craft the approach. Clarity about your vision and mission comes in handy at this point. Understanding the intersection of your short-term and long-term goals provides valuable clarity. And if you've done it well, then you have a vision, goals, and values that provide the foundation for building your team.

Vicki Raimey, sports media leader and teambuilder, remem-bers her approach when she built an intrapreneurial team focused on data at Turner Broadcasting. The trick, she says, is to ensure clarity about your ultimate goal and the skills that will be needed to achieve that goal. From there, she observes that hiring becomes a lot like assembling a puzzle—a variety of different shapes and sizes that will fit together to give you your final result.[1]

How do you find the right people for your team? As Oprah Winfrey has stated, "Surround yourself with only people who are going to lift you higher." This applies from both a business perspective and also a personal perspective.

Further, take a checklist route to ensure you have, as Jim Collins, author of *Good to Great*, likes to say: "the right people on the bus."[2] You want to make sure that you not only have individual capabilities on the team, but also complementary ones that connect to and complement the others as relevant. What are your pivotal roles?

The composition varies, but at minimum, an operating team needs people to fill key roles focused on areas like Product, Technology, Operations, Sales and/or Business Development, and Marketing. These functions contribute directly to the core mission-specific operational work that the intrapreneur needs to do. Here, the intrapreneur has a distinct advantage over the entrepreneur in multiple ways because resources already exist in functions such as Finance, HR, and Legal. The list of important contributors in other roles such as Customer Service and Public Relations can extend a long way also. So please treat this not as an exhaustive list but rather as a sample to build from based on your own needs.

To be clear, you don't always need people who are wholly dedicated to each role all the time—rather it means that there are jobs to be done in each of these areas. Often, intrapreneurs will initially hire in some key roles and "borrow" from the mothership for other functions. To be successful, a project will need dedicated resources in key places over time. You may not get them all at the start of your work. Still, keep them in your plans to be prepared as you expand and grow.

When you've identified the roles needed for your business,

then treat them as essential for success; your project will demand no less. I like to think of the team figuratively (and sometimes literally) as sitting at a large round table. No person or function is more important than any other. Rather, each contributes to the success of the whole, and each can make others at the table more effective.

How many areas of your business do you need each team member to be an expert in? The answer to this question varies based on the situation, including the specific areas of expertise involved.

Often, I want team members who are versatile and can handle a range of responsibilities, especially early on, when the team is small and the jobs are many. This is one area that frequently differs from role definition in the larger enterprise, where each position is often specialized and narrower in scope. This difference makes for some interesting discussions with Finance and HR teams that are used to very precise job descriptions! That said, some spots on any team typically demand deep subject matter expertise. When you identify those roles, you can then hire for these knowledge sets and capabilities without asking those team members to wear many hats—even if it's early in the project's growth process.

A good example of this came during the development of The Weather Channel's first mobile app. We needed experts in mobile product development and technology—actually building the apps. We also needed access to meteorologists, who are experts in our core content area (weather). And each of these individuals did not need to wear many hats. They just needed to be the best at what they did. Were they experts in wireless technology? No. But they contributed beautifully as content experts. They were critical to the team because they could help guide us. But we didn't ask them to play primary roles other than the ones in which they were trained to excel.

Our teams faced similar experiences when hiring some really transformative software developers. Often, time-sensitive projects require using a particular software or applying a high level of software expertise. As a team leader, you'll want to hire for that specific skill set. When timelines are tight on a high-visibility project, there's typically a high premium on deploying a true expert and a correspondingly high cost in cycle time and rework if you're getting a novice up to speed. There are lots of great places for training and development, but this is not one to gamble on if you have the choice.

Still, an intrapreneur should follow broader guidelines when hiring a functional expert. You need more than just their expertise. A successful member of the project will need to embrace the unique demands of an intrapreneurial venture. The key when making these specific skill hires is to understand that your team needs a duality from this individual: the expert must bring the expected topical capabilities but must also be flexible. And by flexible, I mean they must be able to understand the needs of the project and find a way to execute their jobs in that context and in line with team values. It may mean doing things differently from what they're used to or approaching a problem from a new perspective.

If the subject matter expert you hire is the undisputed best at what they do but is entirely inflexible, you're just inviting some serious headaches. An intrapreneur-led project will demand creativity and an open mind. This is not the kind of job where you can simply follow the established rule book. Nor is it one where you have full, unfettered freedom. You can't have your expert crossing their arms and refusing to look for creative solutions. You'll also find frustration if you have a talented team member who has not bought into the vision of the initiative. No one will be happy under those circumstances and your project will have serious unnecessary setbacks.

Be creative in your talent search process. While we've made a significant effort to distinguish between intrapreneurs and entrepreneurs, Dr. Loretta Daniels, an accomplished leader in both for-profit and nonprofit enterprises, suggests that the mindsets of both have very important shared characteristics. In many cases, entrepreneurs can make great intrapreneurs and vice versa, as long as they are able to adjust their style to the environment. You may just need to find them at the right time in their professional development. Understanding where an individual is on their career trajectory and how that person will embrace risk is an important recruiting insight. People are often not fixed in one position throughout their careers. "Intrapreneurs are, at heart, entrepreneurs and risk is just a part of their DNA," Dr. Daniels says. "They are going to be willing to take that risk rather than the easy way out. If they are convinced that this product or service or line of business is going to help this company, they are going to do their research and they are going to take that risk."[3]

This mindset is common ground for both intrapreneurs and entrepreneurs, she says. So, it makes sense for some intrapreneurial team leaders to seek out entrepreneurs who may be ready to engage in building from a different perspective. The payoff can benefit both the company and the team member. Dr. Daniels says, "When you are a person who wants to be independent, who wants to take on the goals of an organization, when you've done it yourself as an entrepreneur, you bring those skills to a company."[4] In other words, intrapreneurial ventures can provide unsurpassed opportunities for entrepreneurs, and entrepreneurial experience can help intrapreneurs accelerate success. The keys include a mindset incorporating curiosity, risk tolerance, and teamwork in a way that applies to your situation.

Additionally, keep in mind that an intrapreneurial team might be the right spot for younger workers. A generational study by WP Engine and The Center for Generational Kinetics found that Gen Z has a strong entrepreneurial bent—with nearly two-thirds saying they plan to start or may possibly start their own businesses.[5] To make corporate life attractive to this generation, larger businesses will need to find ways to embrace and support that creative fire. For many in Gen Z, the opportunity to use innovation skills in an environment where they will have more resources and support to achieve their dreams is an attractive option. This is true in many circumstances, including when they are making a difference for large numbers of people, building a skill set, developing the ability to contribute successfully with larger teams, building financial footing, paying off school debt, and learning from people who can help them advance their careers with a depth of relevant experience. Some of this experience may be functional in nature, and some of it may be related to broader insights into career development and skills that will serve them well in many aspects of life.

Also, intrapreneurial opportunities can provide valuable experiences for interns. An internship helps people develop skills and test their thoughts about what they most want to do with their careers. Especially where there is a good fit, many internships provide lessons that last a lifetime while also resulting in a job offer when the student is ready.

The Power of Differences

The power of differences has been well documented in contributing to stronger financial outcomes. These findings apply to building an intrapreneurial team as well. As you build your team, integrate a search for complementary skills and attributes into your hiring process from the beginning.

This is a great place for an intrapreneur to apply their natural creativity. Of course, consider commonly applied lenses to meet your needs as relevant. But then go beyond that to think about a broader mix of characteristics such as being intentional about having introverts and extroverts, big-picture thinkers and operational gurus, or international and local hires. One fruitful area is a range of age and life experiences—this is especially relevant as we see generational change occurring in the workforce today. Overall, create a team that includes differences in outlook and practice. Look for a skill combination on your team where the capabilities balance and complement each other. This team-building process will help ensure that you don't wind up in a uniform bubble that limits the overall ability to achieve your potential.

A team that includes people with differing perspectives will be a more powerful team, especially if they have a shared purpose and vision to bring them together.

To do justice to this topic, we would need a lot more space and time. I'm not trying to provide a comprehensive guide here. I simply want to emphasize that a broad-minded and genuine commitment to including people with different perspectives pays major dividends in company results, customer satisfaction, team fulfillment, and people development.

Your Boss Matters—a Lot

When you're considering an intrapreneurial role, don't forget to assess the likely fit between you and your boss.

Let's back that one up a minute.

You mean you have some choice too? This isn't a one-way street?

Boss assessment is a critical skill for a successful intrapreneur. It belongs under the heading of "team building" because, for better or for worse, your boss is part of your intrapreneurial team. While you report to them organizationally, your boss is typically not dedicated solely to your venture. However, they play an outsized role in the results you and your team will deliver operationally.

Entrepreneurs don't necessarily face this problem. They are at the top of their food chain. Yes, there's a board, but they are generally the most senior executives in the ongoing operations of the business.

The intrapreneur, on the other hand, works for someone. And that person often works for someone else. Companies have a hierarchy of management you must engage with. To handle this, as you build your team, remember that your boss is part of that team.

You can't always choose your boss. But you can identify whether your boss will be an effective fit for your intrapreneurial team. It also helps to understand your boss's mindset and point of view on your new work.

Ideally, your boss is your sponsor and your advocate. This individual can open doors for you, providing introductions and support. At the very least, you want a boss with key personality attributes such as being secure in their own position and being willing to provide consistent support. A boss who feels secure will be ready to stand behind something they believe in and will not be ruffled by your efforts to create something new. A boss who does not feel secure may see your work as threatening, destabilizing, or distracting while they focus on their own broader needs and reputation in their role.

If you don't have a good relationship with your boss, prepare for a bumpy ride. Maybe not for the business, but likely for you. An intrapreneur takes risks and pushes hard and transforms. And if the boss isn't providing cover, you'll potentially be very unhappy a lot of the time and only marginally successful—or even unsuccessful—some of the time. So, pay close attention going in, and take action accordingly. The converse is true, too: with a strong relationship with your boss, your prospects for fulfillment improve and the outlook brightens for overall success.

Some questions can help you to assess the potential intrapreneurial fit with your boss. Here are some sample questions for you to consider asking them:

- Which elements of this job description are most important to you?

- What kind of organizational support will we have for this business unit internally?

- How would you describe your leadership style in one word? If you had to encapsulate it in a sentence, how would you describe your mission as a team leader?

- Please help me to understand more about your engagement style with team members. How often do you typically meet with direct reports and in what way? Do you prefer agendas or open discussion?

- What was the best conversation you recently had with your own boss? How about the most challenging?

- Have you ever had a boss who was or became your mentor? If so, how did that come about?

- Please share more with me about the most challenging phase of your career and how you grew out of it. Was a manager or boss key to turning that corner?

- When you consider my background and fit for this role, what area will likely involve the biggest learning curve?

- What are your definitions of success in terms of business achievement and relationship quality?

Building the Team

Likely you have the vision of this perfect team in your head. The question now becomes: how do you make it happen?

Some good news is that you've already started your hiring process in a previous chapter. A few pages back, we walk through the process of sketching the values that this project will embody. If you thought that was just an intellectual exercise, now you'll see the values statement as much more than a set of inspirational quotes. The values you listed become the core criteria you refer to in hiring and can act as a central part of the screening process. By leveraging these statements, you can see how candidates will match up against the particular needs of your project—and also the unique needs of any intrapreneurial venture. Often, a resume, references, and even previous experiences together will not surface these important elements alone.

One of my favorite words to include in a project values statement is "curiosity." It can be a big help during the team-building stage. And oh, by the way, as I conducted interviews for this book, curiosity bubbled to the top as the single most consistently identified attribute for effective intrapreneurs.

Let's return to the topic of hiring functional experts. How do you ensure that you're hiring someone who is at the top of their field, while at the same time, open to the flexibility demanded by an intrapreneurial project? Talk about the value of curiosity and bring that in as a core criterion for employment, with the expectation that a strong candidate will provide concrete, compelling examples of it in practice.

Is this individual an inquisitive person? How do they approach problems? Or new material? Or new people? You're looking for that drive, a quality that pushes someone forward into something new. As you interview the candidate or check references, scan for this curiosity factor. You hope to find someone who doesn't just tolerate something new but finds it exciting and enticing. The Java developer who is top-notch in technical ability but thrives on order and predictability may not be your best fit. But the Java developer who describes finding novel solutions to difficult problems or tells you their hobby is cooking and exploring new cuisines or comedy improv may be showing you the kind of curiosity spark that your team needs.

Follow this process with all your values words. If your project values include *openness* or *kindness*, look for evidence that this person practices those values—professionally or personally or both. If you have the word *courage* on your list, in this context look for a resume full of new ventures or innovation accomplishments; watch for public speaking experience, or even commitments like an extended solo road trip. When you keep your values list close, you can use the terms to surface the human elements that will tell you the stories behind the resumes. Everyone can list their skills; you want to know, "Should these candidates with specific skills become my teammates?"

These hiring practices apply in many different situations, not just intrapreneurial ones. However, of all the major attributes one may have, you can focus on a specific subset of them that will yield the highest probability for intrapreneurial success as we note in Chapter 1. Typically, intrapreneurial teams are smaller than others in the organization—sometimes much smaller. Therefore, each team member can make a lasting and disproportionate difference in outcomes.

I want to take a moment to highlight the core value of integrity. Integrity has been a core value of every business venture

I've ever undertaken and had the ability to shape values for. It's a combination of honesty and ethics that matters and leads to strong, evident character in teammates. And this agreement on what matters most plays out in our everyday activities. We want to hire people who live up to the highest values of integrity— even when that means we're taking personal risks to live up to the standards.

It's possible to sustain ethics and excellence while also show- ing respect to the other people involved. This can be as simple as taking a few minutes to gather your thoughts before comment- ing on a controversial or emotionally loaded topic. It can mean having a conversation about a sensitive corrective action with a team member privately instead of in a more public setting. Sometimes, it can involve raising difficult issues and then listen- ing carefully with the intent to understand, instead of engaging in a discussion primarily to advocate for a certain result.

At times, integrity means summoning courage and having hard conversations. This can be very uncomfortable. So, get used to being uncomfortable while also doing your best to take care of the people around you. By doing so over time, you can demon- strate through example the combination of values that yields goal achievement, sustained commitment to team members, and learning along the way.

We're not expecting perfect humans doing perfect work. But we can have the intent to live up to our core values always, and then strive to do this every day.

The values list will also help you pursue what you're looking for in a broader team over time. Hiring a full team all at once can sometimes be ideal. But chances are you won't have the opportunity or resources to staff up in a single sweep. More likely, you'll put your team together in "ones and twos" as an evolution over time. With the values list in mind, you sustain consistency on core characteristics, even as you move forward into the daily scrum of work. When closely observed, centering around values consistently will have a profound effect on hiring and managing a team.

Interview with a Long View

As you build this team, consider the impact each hire will have on the team environment and results. Think of these people you will hire as individuals who will have the opportunity for a long-term relationship with your teammates and you.

This is an important mindset for you as the team leader. Approach the team-building process with the mindset that these can be life-changing relationships. "You always want to work for people who you feel are pulling for you," observes Scot Safon.[6]

If you treat them as temporary and transactional, those around the table will often match your commitment level and work as temps and transactional team members. If, on the other hand, you go in with the commitment level and emotional tenor of someone who expects to engage and value this team for a long time, that deeper investment will come across. You are building relationships with your team members, not just pursuing short-term goals. The people who want to be your true teammates will notice it and respond to it. In an intrapreneurial environment, these relationships can span not only many years but also multiple initiatives as the enterprise grows and evolves.

Communicate this long view to potential teammates—use it

as a recruiting tool. When you can convey accurately to an individual that being on your team will be good for them (in both the short run and the long run), you give them a reason to join you that will be true no matter how an individual intrapreneurial project turns out.

Vicki Raimey learned this lesson herself and applied it to her own leadership process. "My favorite job to this day was for a health and wellness brand that we had for Turner Broadcasting," she says. It was a brand that developed within the sports division. "It was an experimental brand in how we advertised, how we went to market, how we were staffing, what the product was. We were literally crossing all of our brands to create a solution. We were pushing the envelope in ways that we never had before. And we all went into the group knowing it was an experimental brand."[7]

The experience of being on this intrapreneurial team was life-changing for Vicki. "It was energizing. It gave people the opportunity to just ideate and come up with things we'd never come up with before."

They built a memorable environment even though, ultimately, Turner didn't continue the project in this case. "While the brand itself did not survive, we were able to take the pieces and parts and learn from them and reapply them in other parts of the business. It was still one of the best growth experiences and people experiences I'd had. I had management exposure all across the board and I really wish most people could have that type of chance."

This experience became part of Vicki's recruiting mindset: you're not just building a team, you're creating opportunities for your team members to grow.

Also, a note on the nature of these relationships. You're building a professional team. You work actively together based on the shared vision, and then you or they often will move on to other projects. You may be in touch less as other needs move front and center. But do not mistake the transitory nature of a given venture for lack of impact. If you lead the team successfully toward a vision that is meaningful, the process will leave a lasting impression on them and on you. You will come out on the other side changed, and your team members will as well. They will leave with new capabilities and achievements, and with a feeling of having achieved an important purpose. You're creating lasting change in the people with whom you work.

The "Where"—Outside or Inside?

Where will these people come from?

In my experience, the most successful teams for intrapreneurial projects come from a mix of people inside and outside the company, at least after the early gestation stage. You're breaking new ground and trying something creative and disruptive. The idea you're building is often one the company has never tried before. That means you can generate particular benefits by combining people from inside the company with ones from outside the walls to staff this innovative initiative. If you try to build only with people inside the company, you risk insular thinking and delivery. If you try to build only with people outside the company, you risk trying to effect tremendous change without the relationships and knowledge that facilitate the highest success. So, while bringing in outside talent accrues tremendous benefits, solely hiring from outside tends to increase the risk of initiative derailment. While there is no one-size-fits-all approach, as a rule, a mix of inside and outside talent sourcing is ideal.

If you do have a team that comes fully from the outside, it's best to assign the venture a primary contact with high institutional knowledge and credibility to help guide them. If you end up with a team consisting solely of internal team members, make sure to provide ways for them to connect substantively with people from outside the organization as relevant.

To build from scratch, first look inside the company for people who can excel in a different role while already understanding the company's people, culture, and history. I can recall a time when I was starting a new job as general manager of a business, and a technology leader had deep roots within the organization. He was able to teach me how to navigate the company and get things done. Not only did he have a tremendous work ethic, but he also could anticipate needs and resolve issues in ways that few I've ever met could do. We accomplished so much more than if he hadn't been in that role at that time.

But that's not set in stone. The perfect person to guide you through may not be in the company, or they may be there but not available. Access to resources often depends on where you are in a project's growth trajectory. At the start, you likely will have a wish list of more hires, but the budget for only a small number at a time. Still, you need to move forward. Tapping internal talent could be the best solution. Perhaps in the formative stages, you need the skills of an experienced marketer. You may be able to find this talent in-house, rather than hiring from outside.

Also, sometimes you'll have someone dedicated to your line

of business, and sometimes you'll just have fractional time from an individual for your project. You may have heard of those companies that offer fractional services for a wide range of roles like project managers, CFOs, CMOs, and more. The intrapreneur essentially is in the market for services like those with a defined internal talent pool built functionally. So, then you'll be looking for people who can add disproportionate value while minimizing cost. And this effort presents you with a new team-building challenge. The talent and skill you need may be just a few doors down from your current office.

But now, your title has shifted. Instead of being team hiring manager, you are team relationship negotiator . . . or perhaps, the team beg, borrow, and barterer. You're still using your values list as a filter. But now, instead of making a job offer, you're making a slightly different pitch. You need to convince that person—who already has a job—to want to contribute some of their hours to the success of your team. Or, more often than not, you also need to persuade that person's boss that the benefits of contributing to your venture outweigh the costs of adding something new to their plate.

For this reason, one important skill you'll need when amassing a team is relationship building. You may feel like your project is its own universe, but you still exist in the larger ecosystem that is your company. Especially early on, you will need people who work around you to share their resources of time and knowledge. Let's go back to our marketing experts. Perhaps, in the early days of your project, you don't have the need for a full-time hire in the marketing function. But you will likely need some work in this area. Without the resources for a full-time hire, you may find yourself leaning on your company's internal marketing team—looking for someone who can pitch in on the side—until it's too big for that one person to handle and you can then make the case for a full-time marketing hire.

The process of asking someone to share their time with you benefits from a compelling idea and a good relationship. As an intrapreneur, you need to be connecting with people in multiple directions all along the way. You need those relationships for many reasons, and building a team is key among them.

Sustaining the Team

Finally, let's look more closely at a part of team building that is often overlooked in the excitement of the hiring process: keeping the team happy and productive over the long haul.

Team leaders can easily underestimate this mandate. In the exciting run-up of an early-stage project, everyone is fueled by enthusiasm and adrenaline. The promise of a new venture is exhilarating. The chance to disrupt and change an industry is intoxicating. But that feeling doesn't always stay the same. And there will be days, weeks, and months even when the hard work of innovation and change will seem daunting. Because being an intrapreneur inherently involves some major ups and downs, It's Incumbent upon the team leader to ensure that the team is not only built but built to last.

The work of sustaining the team combines emotional awareness and smart practices that reinforce resilience in your team members. You will further strengthen the team by directly connecting to the shared core statements (vision, goals, and values) that enable you to focus on successfully achieving your potential.

Loretta Daniels emphasizes one aspect of team support: celebrating success. This guidance can get lost in the dust flying around a big project, especially at times that involve some serious heavy lifting. Everyone on the team, including those in the larger organization who are watching, may be hyperfocused on the problem the team is trying to solve. "You need to make sure everyone realizes the value they are bringing to the company, even while the work is in progress. And you want everyone around you to know what your team is bringing to the company so they will want to be part of it. People want to be part of a celebration," says Dr. Daniels.[8]

People have written much on team management, and I'll generally defer to that literature. However, I want to emphasize the value of maintaining regular communication with your team members and tracking progress relative to your goals. For my direct reports, I generally prefer to have a scheduled weekly conversation that is partly structured and partly flexible for any other topics that arise. Further, this is a great chance to check on the status of progress versus goals. This may seem like a lot—you have plenty to do and want to empower your team to take care of business without excessive oversight.

In general, I see it as an investment in the person and the business. A lot happens in the course of a week in a fast-moving venture. If you miss a conversation, sometimes the costs of missed opportunities and cleanup for missteps can far outweigh the time commitment you're making with this investment in your team. Of course, as with any guideline, adapt to suit your specific circumstances, from holidays to project status to what overall fosters the best environment.

Additionally, sometimes it becomes clear that team members need more support than usual to be successful. You can help with coaching, development opportunities, and more. Much has been written on this topic alone. It is well worth learning about what options you have here and taking action to continue the growth of each individual. (We cover some ways to do this in more detail later on.) These investments have profound personal and professional benefits in a lot of cases, and a strong larger organization often has many resources to help you help others grow.

Even with those efforts, sometimes you will still find that a team member is struggling in a role. When that happens, you need to find additional ways to maintain expectations while supporting the person to the best of your ability. If you do not do this, then the broader team will feel the effects.

At big organizations, personnel decisions often require more time, care, and preparation than in smaller ones. In a company with many different business units and needs, you also have more opportunities to find a landing place that works better for this individual. If the issues are more about fit relative to the needed skill set, and other teams need this skill set, then you can expand the range of options so that both the individual and the company win. In this case, it is not simply about moving a problem from one place to another. Rather, it is about learning from a situation that did not work and adjusting to find one that does. Regardless, while maintaining a commitment to supporting team members in a range of ways that are appropriate to your situation, you must also ensure you have the right people in the right places.

If you're leading an intrapreneurial team, you will benefit from prioritizing people alignment, performance, and accountability over most other considerations. When you get these things right, many other needed results follow.

Compensation and Benefits

There is no area that illustrates the challenges and opportunities of being an intrapreneur more than compensation (often referred to as "comp"). Intrapreneurial leaders in strong companies tend to have access to an array of tools to support team members—and also limited latitude to change them. Even in the fray of focusing on activities like building products, securing customers, and attending conferences, don't forget that your team members are operating in a competitive talent marketplace. Sustaining a team demands that a leader pays attention to compensation and benefits.

While this book does not seek to cover comp in detail, I do want to make a few comments here. The core components of many comp plans include salary and an annual incentive bonus. For some (mainly in sales), it also includes commissions paid quarterly or monthly.

The importance of salary should be self-explanatory, and the ways to apply it in a larger organization tend to be based on levels (or bands) within a company. These bands generally apply to everyone in important ways. But you may find differences in compensation plan specifics in an emerging business, so handle with care. Where applicable, the annual incentive bonus (in cash, stock, or other units of value) should be enough to motivate each team member—and should be tied not only to mothership performance but also to your venture's performance. If commissions are relevant, the percentage of revenue (or other metric) is also important. It will typically be higher earlier in the development of a business with lower revenue levels, and then decrease as a percentage over time as the revenue base grows. Also, you may have a commission guarantee so that you can secure the talent needed to lift off an emerging business—often as part of a comp plan that is connected to multiple lines of business. In any event, for the purposes of precedent and motivation, variable compensation based on performance is a critical element of the success of intrapreneurial ventures. If you do a great job, you should be rewarded; if your performance is lower, that should be reflected in compensation as well.

Yes, it's important to pay competitively. Companies base compensation plans on market rates. As a corporate player in the industry, you'll have access to information on what salaries are standard and what top talent will demand. As a manager, you can stay informed about if and how the team member's appetite for risk changes over time. Based on this information, you can continue to look for opportunities that optimize the balance between the company's needs and the total compensation package required to motivate talented team members.

One of the best tools an intrapreneur has in some companies is a long-term incentive plan (LTIP) or its equivalent. These plans usually tie a meaningful payout to team members based on the achievement of specific goals. They usually cover a longer period of time by definition—in my experience, at least three years. They can be composed of cash, stock, or both. These sorts of plans provide tangible incentives for a longer-term view and also increase the ability to provide upside in lieu of stock options that are often associated with high-potential entrepreneurial ventures. It's an additional important way for your team to look at the work you're all doing as an ongoing effort, rather than just a "gig."

While abiding by all guidelines related to fairness and equity, my own philosophy is to use the team's compensation resources to reward star performers. As a general rule, I avoid the "peanut butter" compensation approach—that is, spreading it evenly across the team regardless of performance. And I particularly find risks in applying that peanut butter process alone over a period of years. That approach leads to situations where if you get a 3 percent bump in overall resources, everybody gets a 3 percent raise, with no other compensation opportunity, regardless of contribution. Instead of providing an incentive for superior performance, the even spread can reinforce an entitlement mentality. Again, different situations have different dynamics; this is a guideline for intrapreneurial ventures, and not a universally applicable rule.

Whatever your resources may be, ensure that you're doing your best to care for everyone who is contributing to the team, while making reasonable efforts to provide proportionally higher rewards to people who are performing the best. That's when compensation helps the team the most as you build.

The Mindset

Further, don't assume compensation is only about money. People want to be compensated in other less tangible ways too— particularly high-performing team members. Here are some other ways to provide incentives.

- **Give them a challenge.** Make this a mountain worth climbing. Enable your ambitious team members to grow along the way. Foster the behaviors that will enable more success in the process. Some of these types of opportunities involve sharing the vision and plans so the team can connect them with relevant goals and improve your venture in ways unique to them. It also means looking outward from the day-to-day activities and noting the project's potential positive impact on the larger world. Skilled, creative people want to know they can make a difference. Many of the most capable team members have been choosing their jobs and their employers based on a sense of purpose, including an ability to contribute. These opportunities to make a real difference in a values-based environment are part of what a smart intrapreneur offers a team.

- **Invest in their development.** Ambitious people want to become more valuable to their teams and employers. The best training classes help a person develop beneficial skills that last beyond a given engagement. Some focus on hard skills—for example, becoming a better project manager. Some emphasize the softer skills—for example, a program designed to increase leading with empathy. And some are a combination. But all can be valuable, especially if a person is eager to learn. When you invest time and resources in development, you signal to your team that you care not only about daily output but also about the success they will have as individuals, now and in the future. Venture capital investor Paul Iaffaldano points out a specific area of focus to foster innovation and experimentation: "I'm a big believer in using training as a way of encouraging them and giving them positive reinforcement that they can learn new skills and they can learn new things. And so, you need to build a team of people who want to learn new things and think that they are successful when they try and test and learn and try different things. You've got to create that ability."[9]

- **Help them raise their own visibility.** One way to do this is to encourage them to become involved in the leadership of an industry organization. This allows individual team members to shine, and it also increases the visibility of your team and its efforts.

- **Make the opportunity so appealing that they want to stay for growth and fulfillment.** Many people do and should move on from time to time. We want team members to stay as long as a role is productive and fulfilling in multiple ways. And if they leave, it should be for the right reasons—to grow and contribute in a new way—and we should generally celebrate this. Retention of high-performing individuals should be a goal of any leader. I've heard some reservations over time about encouraging your team to take high-visibility roles in wider industry circles. One of the questions that comes up is, "If you do that, aren't you afraid someone else will notice how great they are and poach them?" If you're concerned about that, then look in the mirror. Because it's your responsibility. Part of your job in building a team is to make it a great job with a great company and a great team, so that great people want to stay.

Becoming Your Team's Best Advocate

Remember as you hire a team, that you're not just their leader. You're also your team's advocate in the rest of the company.

This role emerges as a mandate when a project you're working on starts to take hold and show its worth. Everyone at the firm is getting excited about the project, especially when early results indicate that this will be a moneymaker for the company.

A company that truly understands intrapreneurship will often already have a mechanism to provide attractive incentives to people in a growth business. And if not, at this point, you need to join with others including your boss and the Finance team to negotiate so that your team is recognized and rewarded in a way that fits with the larger organization. Often this is very feasible in an innovative company—you just need to put the puzzle pieces together between your venture's needs and the incentive program options your company offers already.

Successful entrepreneurs will often have the opportunity to reap rewards in the marketplace. A public stock offering and other liquidity events can yield financial benefits for those who were part of the early team. In comparison, for many highly skilled intrapreneurs, the compensation and benefits profile is different. The company has put up the funding and support for the project and should receive high benefits for this too. What you want is a mechanism for your venture to contribute to the broader organization in such a way that attractive compensation to the team is clearly in the best interests of all involved.

As your project grows in value, the potential rewards to your team should as well. Sustaining a team is demanding work. Ignoring it means that your top performers will eventually be more likely to get frustrated, be bored, and/or receive a better offer elsewhere and leave. Paying attention yields dividends for the individuals, for the company as a whole, and ultimately for your customers.

The work of sustaining a team continues over time. Your needs will shift and grow. The demands will change and evolve. The people you hire will not stay static, and as their manager, you'll be wise to tune in to what they need to do their best work. The team-building process, no matter how challenging, is also exhilarating. It's the concrete sign that your project is officially out of the starting blocks and racing toward its future.

If you have any doubt about the value of building a capable and principle-centered team, please note the following from Debora Wilson, who led The Weather Channel Interactive business unit and then shepherded The Weather Channel overall through a period of remarkable growth. She says, "I think the extra special magic ingredient is that the leader and the leaders that work underneath that person have got to be trusted by the broader organization. That trust factor is just so important. It allows you to get the hard stuff done and to deliver bad news, which is always going to happen, with credibility."[10] While Debora has had more than her fair share of good news to deliver, she has also had to manage through the ups and downs of multiple growth cycles with very talented teams.

I know from personal experience that she and her leadership team created an environment at The Weather Channel that many associates from that time still describe as one of the best in their careers. I was privileged to serve in the organization then, with responsibility for the mobile team. It was not always easy, and certainly not perfect—and that's normal. All that said, we had the right people working with a strong brand and a great growth business. We learned lessons that we still apply in a range of ways today. And it all started with hiring, nurturing, and aligning disparate team members into an effective whole that applied shared values while feeding intrapreneurial growth.

Chapter Summary

This chapter addresses the concepts an intrapreneur must embrace to build and sustain a team. To make this happen:

- Build intentionally, guided by your goals.

- Leverage the broader organization's strengths when deciding how to staff up, with both dedicated roles and fractional support.

- Build and engage your team as if you are seated at a round table together—literally and figuratively.

- Value differences among people in team member selection, from the beginning.

- Assess the fit between you and your boss.

- Offer an attractive mix of compensation and benefits for a venture of this sort, while aligning it with broader organizational requirements.

- Provide team members with challenges, development opportunities, and broader exposure.

- Foster a team environment that extends beyond transactional needs and offers the potential for relationships that will last throughout the course of a career.

CHAPTER 5

COMMUNICATE WITH CARE, MULTIDIRECTIONALLY

Everyone communicates. In business leadership and management, most people think they have some well-practiced communication skills. It's natural to assume this since we communicate often, by necessity. If we can talk or pick up a pen or put fingers on a keyboard, we're pretty sure we know what we're doing on some level.

And this represents one of the primary pitfalls of intrapreneurship—overconfidence in communications skills. So much so that some people fail to plan and execute an effective communications process from the start, and then they scramble to catch up later.

The hard truth: communication is a pivotal factor in the intrapreneurial process, not just the substance of your idea. Do it well, and your project advances. Just wing it without some serious intentional planning and careful delivery, and you may very well find yourself in hot water, or at the very least, doing a whole lot of unnecessary cleanup.

In this chapter, we look at particular tactics demanded in intrapreneurial communication. After all the effort you've put in thus far, creating a smart communications strategy is worth your time.

These are some best practices in intrapreneurial communications.

If in Doubt, Overcommunicate

Anything with the word "over" as a prefix may sound like a criticism. Overpriced. Overthinking. Overbuilt. But in this case, "over" is exactly what we're going for. It's a big part of the secret sauce in the intrapreneurial communications process. What's more, it emerges as a key place in which many an intrapreneur will stumble.

When you're trying to launch something new and innovative within the walls of a company, your instinct may be to lie low until you have great results to trumpet. Corporate culture often encourages this kind of measured discussion. Don't buy any billboard ads until you can be sure you've got a winner.

But that can't (and shouldn't) stop you from conducting a robust communications process early on. While getting out ahead of your results may be a bit tricky, surprising someone important in your organization can present a much greater risk. Communicating, even at the very early stages, can save you hardship later on.

Here are two examples from my own experience.

In the first case, the economy faced a sudden major challenge right in the middle of the calendar year. Our ad revenues dropped suddenly, and our salespeople relied on commission. Through no fault of their own, their compensation was expected to go down dramatically, just as we were all adjusting to the new environment. Our management team discussed this and decided to address it quickly so team members would not have to worry about changed expectations in financials. We decided to recommend that we pay 100 percent of bonuses to all salespeople for that month while we sorted things out.

Our Finance lead communicated with his chain of command while I coordinated with other leaders, especially those on the sales team. My boss was supportive. Then we got approval back from Finance, had a discussion with our broader sales leadership team, and rolled it out to the entire nationwide sales team. We were quick, decisive, and people-focused while checking with all who needed to be involved. As you might imagine, this was well received. We went through a similar process in future months, managing through until we were able to ease back into a more standard compensation approach months later after we had more of our bearings.

As a second type of example, I've worked with technology development partners over the years that struggled to deliver on time. Sometimes they've been very forthcoming, and in turn, we've done our best to work with them. On the other hand, sometimes they aren't as transparent, which can result in very unpleasant surprises. In the first case (and assuming the partner is a good one overall), that's a fairly standard situation to work through in software development, whether we like it or not. On the other hand, when partners don't communicate, or relay information that turns out to be inaccurate, then the problems become much more difficult. Beyond the operational side of things, the implications are at least two-fold from a communications perspective. First, find partners that will communicate openly and blend this content into your own internal updates. And second, if you end up in a situation where a partner doesn't communicate well, especially about timelines, then go out of your way to dig down to the root of the issues with the partner and also handicap your internal updates with realistic assessments of delivery. This is a common challenge, and if you want to spend less time with some serious explaining to do, then get out in front of the problems with proactive and transparent communication.

Otherwise, the internal friction you experience generally will have limited correlation with the quality of your idea. Rather, it will occur in part because you failed to infuse your project with a robust approach to overcommunication.

This lesson emerges as especially critical for the intrapreneur. Entrepreneurs often benefit from a blank slate. They may have a significant stretch of time to work with before they start talking to a meaningful number of outsiders about plans, while gestating their ideas. But intrapreneurs usually don't live on that timeline. When you're trying to effect change in a large organization, you work in an ecosystem. It may be complex. It may be global. Companies have layers and org charts. They have cultures. Some things are obvious and stated, while other important cultural elements exist as an undercurrent running through the system. The intrapreneur must acknowledge that even if they have a great idea, there are many, many people throughout the firm who have a vested interest in the territory and can block them.

For that reason, overcommunicating (while it may feel as if you're being uncomfortably assertive or repetitive) is actually a smart strategy. You're using communication to build support while surfacing and addressing potential concerns.

Bill Burke likens the necessary communications strategy to the process of sales. When you're an intrapreneur, he says, you're working in sales even if you're not working in sales. That has to be the mindset of your communications process. "You've got to convince other people your idea is a good idea. Your communication needs to be about being optimistic and painting a picture, creating a vision, inspiring people."[1]

Bill recalls using this approach when he and his team convinced Turner Broadcasting to take a chance on creating a new channel, Turner Classic Movies. "It's all about motivating people and convincing them. You need to be persuasive. If someone says, 'What's this all about?' you'd better have an answer. If you don't, shame on you. This is the mandate of internal selling."

When starting a new line of business or other initiative, you'll find multiple strong incentives to having done your homework and developed a clear statement about what your venture is designed to achieve. This incentive for clear and timely communications continues in the operations of the business.

Rusty Friddell, longtime general counsel at Landmark Communications who has been involved in numerous intrapreneurial and entrepreneurial ventures, points out the importance of communication in an environment where team members have wide latitude to make decisions. He says that at Landmark Communications, "there was an unwritten rule that no one would get put in a penalty box if something bad happened." Rather, that was part of the process. However, if it occurred in whatever you were presiding over or working with, you were expected to raise your hand so that everybody could be aware of it, and then support you and try to fix it together as needed. He further observed, "And the two effects of that were, one, you did, in fact, raise your hand when it first started to be a problem. And we could bring in whatever resources necessary to mitigate it and fix it and sometimes turn it into lemonade. But also, you weren't afraid to try things."[2]

The cornerstone of your overcommunication strategy stems from your three-part game plan: vision, goals, and values. You may not have results to share at this early date, but you have your roadmap. You know what you're moving toward, you know why you've undertaken the journey, and (if you've done your homework) you know how to connect it to the larger goals and success of the mothership. You've spent time creating the process and the language of your journey. Now leverage that work—in a wide and vigorous conversation with the many people in your organization who might be impacted by your project. Some of them you will contact because you need their help and their input. Others you will connect with to ensure they don't find out from someone else—risking their taking an instant dislike to your efforts as a result. Investing time to communicate up front is valuable. Missing communication steps can cause costly delays and plenty of angst later. Even if you think you're already stretched with existing commitments, make the time now anyway to bring people into the loop whenever possible.

Start the conversation with your organization, and then keep it going.

Let's look at how to do that in more detail.

Tools

THE OFFSITE

We talked earlier about the value of a sharp, smart SWOT slide. We covered how much impact that one image can have. Well, if a picture is worth a thousand words, a good offsite is worth a thousand slides.

Offsites deliver an opportunity to gather the right people and groups for a conversation. You can present and discuss your concept in detail—not just in the one (albeit excellent) SWOT slide. You can hear their feedback and understand how they view the innovation. Importantly, while making the concept stronger, you can also strengthen support for your team's efforts.

When arranging an offsite like this, strive to keep an open mind about the attendee list. You want to hear from the full spectrum of interested parties. Remember an earlier point: a corporate organization has many parties who might have an interest in your project and any number of them can help or block you.

Communication is a way to get in front of these possibilities and create connections rather than barriers. It's a way to bring them in earlier rather than wait for them to approach you later with their reactions.

When planning an offsite, ensure that you have robust and engaging content. Few things annoy people more at work than sitting through an all-day meeting that's a waste of time. Make sure your presentations are well-constructed and everyone in the room understands why they are there. This represents an opportunity to explain what role you hope others will play in your project. You want everyone in the room to contribute or learn and to feel like they are participating in an appropriate way, not simply showing up as an incidental bystander.

Sometimes you'll barely have a shoestring for an offsite budget, and sometimes you'll have substantial funds to pay for things like a venue, catering, and more. Prioritize getting the participants and content right over a specific type of location. You can get creative on the venue and food to manage expenses. Sometimes you'll even do an "on-site offsite" at one of your organization's own office spaces. Regardless of how you approach the logistics, a space outside of your usual surroundings can produce intangible benefits in the way of creative thinking and interaction. I've seen these events done in our own office space outside of the usual areas, rented offices, innovation centers, business partners' offices, homes, hotels, resorts, and even museums. The key is to make it happen and emphasize value creation and relationship building with your team and any other relevant stakeholders. Good (and great) offsites generate many benefits, and an intrapreneur should include them in the mix.

THE QUICK PING

A quick check-in can be powerful in the intrapreneurial project.

As practical, I reach out to people with specific, brief questions and comments throughout my process. One reason is to "ping" someone in the organization with an introductory thought and to gauge their response.

Hey, I'm playing with this idea about the future of wireless and we're trying to decide if we should build apps or mobile web first. Can you give me your thoughts?

It's important to highlight here that I'm not talking about a particular communication channel. Sometimes this is via text, sometimes it's a phone call, sometimes it's an email, Slack, or other tool. What I want to emphasize here is the concept of the quick ping; I'm not saying how exactly you need to do it. When you reach out in this brief way, sometimes follow-up to the initial outreach will be in another format—such as email or an in-person meeting. But that text is a great tool for many reasons. You're not asking the recipient for buy-in. You're not even asking for a ton of substance at this initial date. You're making the first contact and planting the seed of the idea. How you move forward with this individual will depend on the nature and quality of the response, as well as the other person's level of interest.

As a project moves through its initial stages and you've got a working team, a group text or similar forum makes for a quick and efficient communications tool. Platforms like Slack or other instant messaging programs also help facilitate connection and conversation within a team. While useful in many ways, email is often not quick enough alone for the daily give-and-take a team needs to stay fully connected.

THE SLIDE DECK

Like many other people, I think PowerPoint can be one of the most likely tools to induce eye-rolling in an organization. Here we go again, another long presentation with limited value or snore-inducing content.

I don't like some of the constraints of PowerPoint, nor do I appreciate the distraction that it causes, replacing substantive thought with formatting circuses. I had to be dragged kicking and screaming into the habit of building decks and using them as a communications tool. And I know the pain of sitting through a meeting in which a poorly crafted PowerPoint presentation is essentially holding the whole room hostage. (And by the way, for all the iFans out there, yes Keynote has some nifty capabilities, too, not to mention other options as well.) Still, the idea of a long presentation in any form can make people run for the coffee machine—and stay there!

I know. Really, I do.

But that said, a slide deck typically plays an important role in the intrapreneur's tool kit. Much of the time, it is vital to the communications process.

Here's why:

- **You're speaking to your audience in a familiar way.** Remember, this is not just about your own preferences on how to communicate. Rather, it's about effective communication with the audience. If that's what they're used to, then meet them where they are. And embrace it to capitalize on its advantages.

- **The slide is a forcing factor.** There's only so much you can fit on a slide, and that puts pressure on the creator to be targeted and succinct. In this context, I prefer simple statements and images that convey critical thoughts—ideally between one sentence and one paragraph long, or with focus on a single chart. If the creator can't summarize to this length, they may need to think through the topic more. The PowerPoint slide has limited real estate. It benefits from thoughtful focus.

- **Images and text work together by design.** The software is made to accommodate that combination naturally. Other formats can be more limiting, at least in terms of impact.

- **Videos tell stories.** Videos have an important role when used judiciously and not gratuitously. By the way, a "sizzle reel" can be a great addition to a presentation. This type of video, typically with relevant storytelling and some accompanying audio, can convey core messages and create emotional connections in uniquely powerful ways. But be careful. In intrapreneurial environments, that can also convey that you're spending too much time on the sizzle and not enough on the meal itself.

- **It provides a backdrop for discussion.** No matter how robust your deck is, the real work of many meetings is the conversation. When I've got a ten-slide deck for a sixty-minute meeting, I'm not clicking to the next slide constantly. I like to heavy up on the discussion, knowing that the content is right there in front of the group. It may be the SWOT slide. It may be our vision statement. It may be a graph or chart that conveys valuable research. The prepared info visually facilitates an environment for productive conversation around the room.

This may seem like a lot of work to tell a story, but ensure you do this early in your project. As veteran intrapreneurs will tell you, you'll need these pieces to get your story to take off.

Says Doug Busk, "People call it 'storytelling.' I call it 'story scaling.' Your story should scale. It should draw people in and the story and business case behind it should be eminently share-worthy. That's how you gain evangelists and collaborators."[3]

Derek Van Nostran also points out the importance of consistency and repetition: "This is about aligning to have a clear, consistent message and repeat it constantly. And it has to have you as a leader, as well as your team, saying the same things in the same way and saying it to as many people within the organization as possible. This way everyone is aligned on it within your team on what you're trying to accomplish, and everyone is aligned outside of your team as to what they believe you are accomplishing."[4]

CONVERSATIONS

I can't stress this one enough. Individual and small-group conversations are critical to the communications approach of an intrapreneur. This observation may sound self-evident, and yet you might be surprised to find how many people underestimate it. Some people perceive that they're too busy or have more important things to do.

If you're mapping out a communications plan that emphasizes technology and puts conversation way down the list, you are headed for trouble. We organize companies to deliver products and services to customers. We construct them to make money and advance professional goals. But they are also filled with human beings. Most of the technology in the world is created to foster connection with and deliver other benefits for people and the world around us. As we do this, we can't forget our original tools: the way we talk with each other.

A conversation may sound more informal than written communication, but an intrapreneur must approach conversations thoughtfully. While authenticity, speed, and agility have important roles, so do presence and situational awareness. Sometimes, careful prep is needed for simple conversations. And the environment matters.

To stay in the right conversation zone as a leader in a corporate environment, I've developed guidelines including this reminder: You are not a basketball coach. Yes, I realize, the basketball court environment is typically a lot different than the typical conference room.

So, what does that mean? I'm a big fan of basketball, especially college basketball. Some of the coaches in this sport are legendary and have a very direct communication style. This is on display regularly during the basketball season. But there's a big difference between the typical communication approach that a hoops coach uses on the court and the demands of an intrapreneurial leader in a meeting room.

If you're a coach standing on the sidelines and see a player doing something that needs to change, you can call it out right then and there. If the player didn't follow the plan, you might get in front of them and say something like, "You drove to the basket when we talked about staying outside. Staying outside is the plan. We need you to get back in there and stick with the plan."

That's typically fine for a basketball court—many coaches, players, and fans would certainly tell you so. But it can be problematic in a corporate setting, especially in companies in which cordial interaction stands as the organizational norm. A basketball coach can serve as a model for intrapreneurs in many ways, but a direct copy of an on-the-court communication style in a corporate team meeting can result in challenging team dynamics.

Every organization has a culture. This is often a key point of difference between intrapreneurs and entrepreneurs. In an entrepreneurial setting, you might hear a lot more open disagreement. There may be an environment that values conflicts, vigorous debates, thrown chairs, and food fights (well, at least the conflicts and debates). Entrepreneurs don't always lie awake at night thinking about how they can possibly win congeniality awards. There's an expectation and acceptance of wider ranges of behavior at times.

Intrapreneurs may face very different cultural expectations.

Some larger companies *are* boisterous and have that level of in-your-face engagement. But a lot are not, and often, the older and more established a company is, the quieter the hallways have become. There is a certain expectation that everyone will be nice to one another. So nice, in fact, that important things may not be said. That means, if you opt to criticize someone directly in a meeting or another public setting, you may find the ripple effect jarring. In some of the companies that I'm familiar with, someone who received a sharp comment in a meeting might be torn up over it for weeks or longer—regardless of the merit of the comment.

Therefore, the communication style I now strive for when leading in an intrapreneurial setting includes this broad (and not always literal) guideline: you're in a meeting room, not on a basketball court—act accordingly. Regardless of whether the intrapreneurial team is interacting in person, virtually, or by written communication, the same concept applies. While the expected behavior differs by setting, the desired outcomes such as work excellence, tangible results, superior teamwork, and individual growth remain the same.

This is an especially important lesson for the intrapreneur. If our values include respecting people, then at the core, we want people to see this in our actions and to feel cared about generally. We will typically be more effective when behaving in culturally acceptable ways. We can't make people happy all the time, but we can make extra efforts to show that we appreciate them. Someone in the organization who feels like they have been addressed in a disrespectful way can generate unnecessary friction and negativity. And this is true even if all the original intent for everyone involved was positive. I, along with many people I know, have forgotten this lesson occasionally, and as a result, we have dealt with the fallout of a single comment for a long time afterward. Please learn from our mistakes and handle with extra care!

If you remember that you're in a meeting room and not on a basketball court, you will address some challenging issues differently. You might make sure to affirm the person before tackling the issue diplomatically. Where the company culture and situation require it, you might meet privately with someone instead of being direct in a meeting. You can then discuss that person's concerns and walk through their needs to drive new actions. Sometimes, if you handle these types of conversations privately and add a bit of authentic support to the discussion, you can achieve the same result while redirecting the individual's behaviors positively. And this landing place is important: we're not talking about avoiding issues. We're talking about dealing with issues directly and effectively but with less friction and in a more collaborative work environment.

If you choose to speak sharply with someone from the figurative meeting sidelines, you can spend far too much emotional and professional capital trying to clean up the mess.

As an intrapreneur, you are not a basketball coach. You also do not get the latitude of some entrepreneurs in this context. Conduct yourself accordingly in your communications. If you forget, someone may quickly and unpleasantly remind you.

Tom Daly[5] has the following advice for intrapreneurs regarding communications:

Tom's Tip No. 1: Don't use politics; use diplomacy. Too many intrapreneurs think they need to end-run or corral or otherwise outwit people who oppose them. But Tom says instead of relying on politics, intrapreneurs should try diplomacy. "I share my working definition of diplomacy; I didn't make it up. . . . Here it is: diplomacy is the skillful reconciliation of incompatible narratives. That's the answer to the question. I want to go left. You want to go right. How are we going to bridge that gap? All that goes back to persistence and patience and diplomacy. That's politics but in a good way."

Tom's Tip No. 2: To introduce a controversial point, look for commonality. To illustrate this, Tom harkens back to his days at Coca-Cola. Tom wanted to get his fellow leaders excited about mobile. In the early days of mobile technology, it seemed like an attractive channel for connecting with customers, but some were skeptical that this technology channel would have a role in consumer products like soft drinks. To make his case, Tom framed the idea in beloved Coca-Cola concepts.

> We had to find that common cultural reference point, the internal company reference point. We needed to link it to something that everybody in the company already knew. Something they couldn't question. So, I went with the notion that everyone in the company knew: Coke wants to put its brands within arm's reach of desire. Nobody there would argue that. That's the concept I used—except at the end of that arm, between it and desire, is a mobile phone. Our choice is whether we want it to be a barrier or an enabler. And at that point, no one is going to argue. There's zero arguments. We all understand the common cultural point of being in arm's reach of desire.

Communicating with the Boss

Which tool should you use to keep your boss updated? Text? Email? PowerPoint? Conversation?

The right answer to that is: whatever method your boss likes best. And that almost always will include a mix of options depending on the situation. Of course, there's some discretion involved here, and it's a two-way street. However, the goal of communicating effectively is primary.

If you think presentations are great to unveil ideas but your boss prefers an email preview first, adapt. If you're an avid texter but your boss prefers a conversation, make it happen. Some bosses like a weekly face-to-face meeting (in-person or virtual). Some lean more on written updates with fewer scheduled discussions. Some just want higher-level summaries most of the time, and others have deeper interest in detail. In any event, maintaining an ongoing flow of communication *with* (not just *to*) your boss is critical to intrapreneurial success.

Since it's likely that you won't get a blank check to follow your plan without routine approvals (approvals that actually can have their own benefits in terms of improved results and buy-in), upward communication in the organization will be an important part of your process. And by the way, a good boss is not just an approver, they also help to make your good ideas better and your actions more effective. The best bosses are success magnifiers, not success inhibitors.

Use these communications not only to keep your boss in the loop but also to understand how your project is faring in the wider corporate landscape. If your boss wants what seems to be A LOT of communication—or conversely, what seems to be very little of it—this may be a red flag for you. A boss that must know every detail, every day, may lack confidence in what you're doing. That boss may be creating corporate quicksand to slow you down or even sink your effort. At the same time, a boss that never wants to hear from you may not be invested enough in your success. You can learn a lot about how your project is faring by paying close attention to the communication requests from your boss. You can then use this insight to ensure that you stay on top of current opportunities to deliver on goals and link your project to the overall company's needs.

Tailored Communication and Engagement

You often need to adapt your message and style for different people and groups, even if you're covering the same topic. Across the organization, team members have different needs in their respective roles. As relevant, you will want to offer answers to the questions they naturally have, insight into important aspects of your initiative, and clarity about their role in the process. By doing so, you can more effectively align the many people who affect your success.

The stakes are high with your communication, including clarity about who is responsible for what within your venture. Seasoned media and technology leader Joe Fiveash observes the following:

> If you've got to get something out of the ground, then you need the hearts and minds of a whole bunch of people

and you need to paint it in vivid colors and include others in this idea that you're gonna go change the world. So, the first part is to be aspirational. And then on the execution side, I certainly feel really strongly that everybody needs to understand who owns what, and that there's nothing that drops in the middle and it's like, 'well, I thought you were doing it' or 'it's not my job.' It's important to have those lanes. But it's also just as important that everybody understands that the team succeeds if there's success and the team fails if there's failure. And so, if you have a bunch of people who don't care about what's happening outside their lane, then it will never work.[6]

A common way to think about the general roles is with a RACI chart. RACI is an acronym that identifies four basic types of roles stakeholders have in an organization, which are based in part on an overview in Forbes Advisor:[7]

- **Responsible.** This is the individual tasked with doing the work and completing the assignments. Every task should have at least one Responsible person assigned to it. It's fine to have more than one Responsible team member per task.

- **Accountable.** This is the individual with a wider view of the task timeline. This person makes certain that every Responsible person knows their role, their expectations, and their deadline. Every task needs just one Accountable team member.

- **Consulted.** These are individuals whose work will be impacted by the outcome of the project. They are asked for feedback and input while the project is in progress.

- **Informed.** These individuals need to be updated as work progresses, but they're generally outside the ring of active project participants and decision-makers. They may be in different departments and may be affected by the outcome of the project.

By applying the RACI framework, you can better understand what each person needs in order to reach the desired outcome. This approach acknowledges these different needs and roles; it is very consistent with the Platinum Rule: treat others as *they want* to be treated.

BE A GOOD LISTENER

What's the biggest mistake an intrapreneur communicator can make?

Hint: we haven't discussed it here yet. It's not too much or too little outbound communication. It's not creating a one-hundred-slide PowerPoint presentation for a one-hour situation assessment. It's not even some imperfect work on team roles.

All of those missteps can be fixed—sometimes easily and sometimes with more effort and thought.

The biggest mistake an intrapreneur can make in communications is being a poor listener. If you are not a good listener, you will likely not be a successful intrapreneur.

Being a good listener is not easy. It's not simply a function of being quiet while the other person is speaking. Being a good listener demands that you engage with the speaker, even when you are not talking. It's about absorbing what is being said to you and understanding what that person needs to hear from you—and what your project needs in the context of this conversation. It's being curious and really wanting to understand.

It can be hard.

If you've had a long day of too many meetings, you're already thinking ahead to the next one, and you're not really present in the conversation, the other person can tell. It comes through quickly when you discuss something important, miss key content or signals, and then receive a very strong reaction from your conversation partner. You often know right away. This is a pitfall you want to work actively to avoid. If you're not actively listening, you are placing your project in jeopardy.

The best intrapreneurs I know consistently listen well. They make a commitment to be mentally and emotionally present no matter what. Even if they're dealing with a major operational issue. Even if they've got a team member with a serious performance challenge. Even if they just found out their child got sent to the principal's office today for misbehaving. Those intrapreneurs sit and engage with the person in front of them. Because whatever else is going on in their day, the person in the conversation with them at this moment expects them to be present.

This is a critical mindset. In the moment, it fosters clear communication among team members. The individual speaking with you is confident you are hearing what's being said and that you'll take appropriate next steps.

But it's also an important way to put deposits in the relationship account. You have a relationship with whomever you are meeting. It may be a new relationship. It may be one that lasts for years and spans many projects. But a conversation is part of a relationship. Being present in the moment is a great way for you to convey to the other person they are valued. And people remember when they feel valued by you. Think of it this way: if you go back to that individual one day and need something, and that person thinks, "Yeah, I remember when I was meeting number fourteen on his big day, and he was totally checked out." Will this person feel valued as a result of this conversation? Likely not. Will you have learned from the valuable things they may have said? Good chance they were missed. Will you get what you need? Maybe not as well. Listening well improves relationships and outcomes.

Ultimately, the way you communicate will create the ecosystem for your project. The words you use, the tactics you employ, the listening skills you practice consistently, and the conversations you inspire will move out into the rest of the organization and act as the backdrop for your efforts. So, choose your words—and your other communications tools—wisely. They matter.

Chapter Summary

You may come to this book with strong business communication skills, but this chapter highlights the important ways that intrapreneurial communication can be different.

- Communicate in a timely way to ensure the right messages get to all necessary parties. If in doubt, overcommunicate, and speak up sooner rather than later.

- Employ a tailored mix of communication options including offsites, quick pings, presentations, and conversations to achieve your team's goals.

- When guiding team members in a corporate environment, remember you're a leader in a meeting not a coach on a basketball court. If you forget, prepare for the cleanup effort.

- Understand the RACI model to tailor communication to different people and groups.

- Practice and model excellent listening skills. Too often, intrapreneurs are so enthused about a new project, they fail to slow down to hear the important conversations around them.

CHAPTER 6

ACTIVATE
YOUR BUSINESS

I could write an entire book about how to activate a new business. Indeed, many authors have already done this. The process and pitfalls of general business building have been well-documented.

In this chapter, we go into very specific territory—how to activate a business as an intrapreneur. The activation process differs when you're doing it from within the walls of an existing enterprise. It also differs from the experience of growth when you're out in the world on your own and are free from a parent company's corporate expectations. An entrepreneur typically also operates independently from the support—both financial and institutional—that corporate ownership provides. So, for better or worse, the intrapreneur has a distinct experience, and that experience demands some different behaviors and expectations than we can glean from the entrepreneurial set.

We start with products and technology.

Develop Products

When you're an intrapreneur, you're not the only one in the broader organization working on innovation. Indeed, in a healthy company, value creation occurs in multiple places, in different departments, and at different stages. Developing new products is the lifeblood of many firms. Companies that don't inject innovation into their ongoing business activities are eventually destined to fail or, at best, succumb to mediocrity.

As an intrapreneur, your innovation will coexist with other intrapreneurial initiatives, and you can harness the broader capabilities and history of the organization for help. In many cases, those creating new products will be taking a creative turn on existing lines of business. Here's a good example of this: Netflix. Netflix started in 1997 as a service for viewers to receive DVDs by mail. And then in 2007, they started Video on Demand. Streaming involved a completely different delivery model and was very disruptive—as accounts of this company's history attest. However, at the core of it, they provided a service so viewers could watch videos in their own homes or on the go. Therefore, the new business demonstrably aligned with the core value proposition of the company, even as technology and viewing trends changed. This serves as a prime example of intrapreneurial opportunity. However, the delivery on market promise varies widely based on how well the company can identify relevant opportunities and then excel at delivering on its potential.

Intrapreneurs sometimes must start by staring at a blank page. And yet you have resources from around the company at your disposal. As many people have observed, the magic often happens when you act entrepreneurially while harnessing the power of the company overall. The Weather Channel launched weather.com in 1995 and expanded the digital business from there. In 2001, the desktop website was growing, and we were also on a journey to create a new app for phones. Now, I know it's hard to imagine given the current state of technology, but at the time, most mobile devices could only handle text. We had "candy bar" phones (so named because of their shape) and flip phones. And they were mostly used for, well, talking!

However, mobile data was growing rapidly. The most common type of usage revolved around text. Cool, I can actually send a message without talking with someone—with plans for dinner, or breaking news. Or a weather forecast. Then phones gained more capabilities, including images for the first time. The screens presented black-and-white or grayscale images. Not the fancy high-quality graphics of today.

In our company, we realized we had the opportunity to provide a new dimension to the experience—radar maps that told so much about what was going on beyond the daily or hourly forecasts. So, when we decided to create a new product with them (radar maps for mobile phones), no one had any framework we could embrace as a foundation. The screens were about the size of a postage stamp, and the images were still very basic. We had to build our own product requirements. We didn't have an existing set of specs to refer to. Radar maps for mobile presented an entirely new opportunity on this platform.

As a result, and even though a broad and talented team contributed, a large portion of product development work for this project concentrated on two of us—a very talented product manager named Irene, and me. We learned a lot from a range of our teammates at weather.com and The Weather Channel network, particularly how they deployed images on other screens. We learned from meteorologists what would be relevant. We learned from wireless carrier counterparts what the phone specs were. And then we just figured it out.

I distinctly remember sitting in a conference room on the eighth floor of The Weather Channel's building with Irene as we were deciding what maps would be useful to viewers. While a single image was a possibility, we wanted to have multiple levels of resolution or many miles covered. And we didn't know how to do it at first. You couldn't pinch and zoom on the screen. Rather, to zoom in and out, you just used number buttons on a phone screen that weren't that far removed from the old touchtone phones—just smaller. We had a deadline and needed to complete the product specs. So, we played with a range of ideas and came up with a simple approach that had some logic to it. We decided the lowest helpful resolution was seventy-five miles. Three hundred miles was about ideal, and we could provide the big picture up to twelve hundred miles. So, we implemented five levels of zoom starting at seventy-five miles and then doubled it each time—to one hundred fifty, three hundred, six hundred, and twelve hundred miles successively. Each of these layers of zoom required retrieving an image from a server. It sounded reasonable on paper, and then we experimented with our technical team. After some adjustments, it worked, and we had a new product feature that turned out to be one of the most popular ones on that app—not to mention photogenic enough to put on the outside of new phone boxes along with our logo for marketing in stores.

When you're building a product, sometimes you're also building its demand. Communications and marketing executive Katie Klein had that experience when she was part of AT&T's intrapreneurial team called Digital Life. This particular effort was new territory for the company. "We were building this new product set for them. And I'm leading marketing and then advertising for that group."[1]

So much of Katie's work revolved not just around creating a product, but also creating its customer base. "A lot of what we were doing was really building out the demand for Digital Life, and the partnerships around our sales channels to support it. And I spent a ton of time advocating and trying to get us in the presence of retail and indirect partners." The team was building awareness and distribution in tandem.

This section on products just scratches the surface of how to approach product needs in an intrapreneurial company. A wide range of resources exists on how to excel at product management. Frankly, many companies have plenty of room for improvement to do this. To do it well, and in addition to any resources you may already have access to, consider learning more from experts like Marty Cagan, a founder at Silicon Valley Product Group.[2] They offer guides focused on developing product excellence and sustaining it over time.

Establishing the Technical Infrastructure

Technical infrastructure occupies a primary role here because it fundamentally affects capabilities and differs so markedly from the entrepreneurial experience. Tech entrepreneurs in today's marketplace often bring technology expertise themselves. Many of the entrepreneurial innovations in our era emerge from tech centers around the world, and innovation is driven by leaders with backgrounds in software development and other technical skill sets. So, when the time comes for a modern entrepreneur to build out the initial technical infrastructure, the steps are generally clear. This is a job for many an entrepreneur's existing peers in the larger technology ecosystem.

Chances are good that the leader of this new business has access to the talent they'll need from an extended network. Maybe they can even recruit previous coworkers, classmates, or others within a group of people who have already exhibited talent and success in their focus areas. The talent pool in parts of the entrepreneurial world has quite a bit of crossover. Skilled individuals will move in and among many of the same companies and social groups.

The intrapreneur works within the walls of an organization. Regardless of where team members are based and regardless of the level of technical training and experience, the intrapreneur can look in multiple directions to find the talent needed to build a growing enterprise. First option: work within the existing IT framework of the company. This demands a close relationship with leadership in IT. You're asking for that department's time, effort, and resources. You're building something new, but you're doing it with potential access to existing capabilities. The guardians of those capabilities must be fully on board with your mission and vision to maximize success.

If you opt for the internal path to access tech resources, be prepared to manage the resulting and predictable reactions. This path can generate a lot of attention within the walls of the firm. Many people, both inside and outside of the technical team, will know you're engaging existing IT resources. You should also be prepared for news to spread quickly as to how well early prototypes are performing. Sometimes, IT specialists assigned to your project will have responsibilities elsewhere in the firm. Information will seep out. That can be good or bad depending on how well early efforts play out. If your first steps are successful, your project's momentum will likely build quickly. But if there are some initial false starts, that will be shared as well. Working with internal IT demands an additional layer of communication management on your part. Information tends to travel fast for initiatives unless they are specifically protected with effective levels of confidentiality during their development.

Alternatively, you might consider outsourcing sizable portions of your technical platform construction. This is especially true for specific purposes where you don't have the expertise and tech already internally, but another company offers it externally. I followed this path routinely. In many cases, the business our team was proposing was so new to the company that we simply did not have the expertise we needed within the walls. We were building something for the organization requiring capabilities and infrastructure that didn't yet exist.

Sometimes, you have to travel one primary path to realize you really ought to travel the other one, at least over time. At The

Weather Channel, we largely built early app offerings using technologies such as Java and BREW with outsourced providers, years before the iPhone and Android apps arrived. Later, it became clearer that we would want more control and flexibility with our offerings, and so we gradually moved development in-house.

Outsourcing brings its own set of issues. They include the following:

- Securing the financial resources required to fund and sustain the effort.

- Relying on another company's platform and related development timeline when this platform is used to service multiple clients. These multiple clients have diverse requirements, and so your service provider must juggle these priorities. Your company will rarely receive the full support you want, when you want it, and for a price that fits your budget.

- Relying on team members at another company. The service provider is subject to the same forces in the job market that many others are, and they can lose key employees at critical times—with you having little recourse until they fill the gap.

- Changing priorities in a successful relationship. A stellar partner may establish such a strong reputation that they become an acquisition target. When in acquisition talks, partner companies can do things that impede your progress—like having distracted executives and making major road map adjustments. If and when an acquisition is completed, the attention to pre-deal clients can change dramatically, especially if the company is absorbed into a larger company with even more clients and priorities. By the way, sometimes the opposite happens, and an acquired company receives the resources and attention it needs to grow even better with you.

So, while you can achieve more results in less time and fewer long-term capital commitments with external tech, you also trade out control and flexibility to manage your own enterprise needs.

Just because you're working with outsourced tech talent does not mean that you can ignore efforts to build a strong relationship with your in-house IT team. Indeed, your relationships with outside technology providers surface a discrete set of issues that you'll need to address with your company's technical leadership. If the mothership IT leadership sees you as a security threat or an imposition to their already overburdened team, you will find your outsourcing efforts burdened by internal dissent. Even when you engage outside resources, remember to build your relationships and maintain your communication inside the organization.

In any event, some broad IT requirements will typically apply to you. These include enterprise tools (including human resources and communications systems), cloud storage agreements, and security protocols. These requirements actually come with benefits and can serve as a strong differentiator for your business if well managed.

Ultimately, it helps if your team has one primary individual responsible for maintaining your connection and positive relationship with the broader organization's technology leadership. I recall that upon my arrival at CNN, the company had dedicated only two full-time people to the mobile team—a remarkable team member with this type of role and me. But Mark had been at CNN for many years. He had the depth of knowledge and experience to provide great context. He knew who the best people were. He knew how to have backchannel conversations that prevented forest fires. It was like having a sherpa to lead me through the new territory of technology there. And his abilities to act as a guide and provide that institutional knowledge were instrumental in getting our new intrapreneurial business off the ground.

Build and Implement a Marketing Plan

Start working on your marketing plan early. If you wait until the product is perfectly polished and out to the customer, you may be too late. At the very least, you can miss important opportunities to meet customer needs and communicate in target markets.

Two reasons to start early: marketing will help you test your concept, and it will help you align with the larger corporate brand.

TESTING

You don't want to spend a year developing a product and then find it's failing because customers don't want it. We live in a world that demands speedy iteration in so many cases. One way to gain confidence in your next iteration is to reach out and see

how your product is experienced by current or potential customers. You want to test your message, your customer appetite
for the product, and the early response to its use. This need for
testing leads many people to open up a channel and begin connecting with their customers. But often not all customers or
all at once. Sometimes, you only expose the content to a small
group in a private setting. Early activation may call for a staged
roll-out of the messaging and product. But you're ready for the
first stage of outreach.

Take this critical step, even if it feels early. You can do all the
research you want, but the true test of any product's viability
comes in the hands of customers. The marketing plan should
start early and then grow and iterate with the product itself.

Finally, the inclusion of marketing at this stage serves as a
forcing mechanism: it encourages the team to look outward to
the customer and ensure the product is not just new and not just
innovative but focused on meeting a customer need. When you
launch your product in the marketplace, the reality that there is a
customer on the other side of this new product or service comes
into sharp focus.

CONNECTION TO THE BIG BRAND

If you're working within a big company, your product is housed
within the framework of an existing brand—perhaps one that is
well-known and respected by many people. Your initial marketing helps you to align with the larger brand. The intrapreneur
can often leverage the power of this existing corporate brand,
either publicly or in business-to-business conversations. As you

activate and begin the marketing process, you can look for ways to connect your initiative to that customer and marketplace brand equity.

Plan this particular part of the process carefully—a misstep could be costly. The team running the existing brand's marketing efforts will not look kindly on an internal upstart that undermines their strategy. So, the intrapreneur must tread with care here. That said, the opportunities are also stunning. If that internal upstart could be complementary and supportive, that helps to get a nod—and perhaps even additional support. As an intrapreneur, crafting your early marketing messaging to support and strengthen the mother brand is a smart strategic move.

Prove Financial and Strategic Viability

The time has come to put some real numbers on the board. At the activation stage of a business, you will need more than your SWOT slide and your plans; you will be asked to start proving that your concept is viable. For that, you need to test, measure, and learn.

To do this successfully, maintain your flexibility. When converting your plans into reality, you may find they don't play out as expected. In fact, this kind of change is the norm. When reality hits, the intrapreneur must be ready to adjust. Back at The Weather Channel, from an earlier experiment, we had boxes of branded pagers sitting in a storage closet. Good idea to try, but not adopted at scale. The marketplace didn't take to them as we had hoped. However, that experiment provided useful information about one approach that didn't work and gave us some signals about what to try (or not) next. In the first days of early mobile data, we were still looking for the best form factors, content, and products. Clarity increases as you begin the activation and hard numbers come in. These empirical experiments provide valuable data that you'll be asked to use to prove financial and strategic viability.

Navigating the Corporate Matrix

How can you avoid stepping on land mines as you traverse the corporate landscape? This topic comes up all the time for an intrapreneur, so let's talk about how it plays out during the business activation phase.

While continuing to introduce change, this is a point when it is best to engage the relevant people in your organization in new and impactful ways. You can disrupt while also finding ways to align with relevant teams in the broader organization. It's a balancing act—and those who do it well can go far. Now, you represent a real product and a real entity within your firm. But you may still have limited credibility, little to no revenue, and a relatively tiny team that seems to be everywhere, all at once, asking for corporate resources.

How do you navigate this precarious stage?

Business builder and insurance expert Lee Scoggins offers these tips for bringing the organization along with you:[3]

1. Ensure you have stakeholder alignment. To get this you can:

   a. Have the owner/CEO involved

   b. Demonstrate that people are buying the product with early success

2. Show compelling value.

   a. Demonstrate return on invested capital (e.g., pre-selling to bring in three new customers, demonstrating it generates revenue)

3. Effect process and operational change to support the new initiatives.

One of the best approaches connects back to the teambuilding stage. You can gain a lot of internal credibility if you've got a serial intrapreneur on your team.

Now, serial entrepreneurs have received lots of attention. These include people in innovation hot spots and beyond who seem to have a crystal ball. They appear to live on the leading edge of trends. They cycle through innovation after innovation, sticking around for a limited time at their creations and often visibly cashing out and moving on.

For our purposes, I'm focused more on the serial intrapreneur—the team member who has walked the corporate halls and innovated from the inside. Maybe it's you and maybe it's someone else who can help you, big time.

These people exist. In any successful company, you will find the innovators—and you will likely find that they are not one-hit wonders. These are internal change agents who have managed to do this multiple times. It helps to have a serial intrapreneur pitching in on your team, both for that person's creativity and for their ability to handle corporate scrutiny. These veterans can walk the halls with no revenue and no history for the current initiative, and yet, they radiate credibility because they've done things like this before. They see around walls and generate trust based on their successful track records with other products. Your effort can benefit from that trust until you have your own numbers to put up on the board for all to see.

Rinse and Repeat on Successive Iterations

Innovation demands iteration. On this, both the intrapreneur and entrepreneur face a similar mandate.

Eric Ries popularized this concept with his Lean Startup movement. The goal: get the product out in the marketplace and use the feedback to create a new version as quickly as possible. We can repeat this cycle many times before the best possible version of the product is achieved. It's the way consumer technology innovation has been emerging for years. Anyone who owned an original iPhone can attest that ongoing iteration makes a good thing better. With each version, the product is improved thanks to in-house experts and consumer comments. The ecosystem of the product benefits from broad use to make the product better in each subsequent generation. You might care about some improvements more than others, yet they are part of an overall evolution where the next layer builds on the previous ones.

This observation applies to software as well as hardware. With a range of products and services, we continue to receive reminders to download software updates. They come from the work of product teams near and far, observing how the product functions in the real world and taking that information back to the lab to update and improve.

But while this process benefits both intrapreneurs and entrepreneurs, many entrepreneurs have a higher comfort level with the cycle. The entrepreneurial world accepts and encourages the "fail fast" methodology. Entrepreneurs are often comfortable with bigger bets relative to their size on a relatively short cycle time. It's the nature of their regular landscape. Their world brims at times with brash projections and wild leaps of possibility.

Intrapreneurs face a different landscape. As corporate employees, their regular roles often abound with incremental upgrades and iterations on a longer cycle time. Proctor & Gamble built a global empire on that very process. The history of product development within the corporate structure is not one that traditionally includes the word "fast." Indeed, the history of great corporate innovators often involves years-long development stories that preceded a product launch. The backstories of firms like Bell Labs and General Motors are filled with innovators who spent great swathes of their careers on a single product.

While "fast" does not always bubble to the top of the traditional corporate lexicon, neither does the word "fail." Indeed, if you polled corporate workers today, you'd find they have a healthy avoidance of that word. Traditionally, if you failed in a project in the corporate world, you would not receive a pat on the back and encouragement to try again. In the old days—and not that long ago, mind you—you might well be fired. Certainly, you could suffer reputational damage. And yet, innovation involves experimentation and some amount of failure, with valuable learning accruing along the way.

Digital sports media veteran Manish Jha observes that many large companies will try to have every aspect of their company perform.[4] They may even keep failing businesses just to avoid the appearance of failure. This contrasts sharply with his experience in the entrepreneurial world, where there's an acknowledgment that some businesses will not succeed as part of ongoing innovation.

So, while the process of "try, fail, learn, repeat" (to accompany successes along the way) is one that must be carried out in the intrapreneurial space, you'll need courage to overcome the old mindset of self-protection versus innovation.

Successful iteration with new ideas goes back to selection of team members and the shaping of team culture. You need skills on your team, and the relevant mindsets to engage in this necessary learning process. You need team members who won't become attached to a single way of thinking. They must see reality in the first round of feedback and make changes if necessary. If the creators at Microsoft had resisted feedback, we'd still be dealing with Clippit, the infuriating virtual office assistant that popped up every time we opened our laptops. No doubt ol' Clippy seemed like a good idea when first launched. After all, the feature was designed based on research, with the intent to help customers. But when customer feedback was negative, the Microsoft team heard that and made the pivot. Successive iterations of the Office software were Clippit-free (with the exception of a few self-deprecating spoofs in their advertising). Microsoft showed in its actions and marketing that it could hear and respond to the marketplace.

In addition to having the right teammates in other places, success in the iteration stage also benefits from having a supportive boss. When early feedback comes in neutral or negative and changes are needed, the intrapreneur will want a boss who provides air cover. If your boss can't shield your team from the inevitable headwinds around the office halls while sharing valuable supporting perspective, then the product may never iterate at all. It may simply wither.

This is another reason for choosing the right boss. When you set out on your intrapreneurial adventure, imagine how your boss will react if the product launches and the comments section starts to fill up with negative reviews. How will they behave? That's important to consider ahead of time. You don't want to find out in the moment that your boss is the kind of leader who will step back and let you take the flack alone.

Be a Humble Explorer, Backed by a Brand and Resources

Finally, let's talk about the role of attitude in the activation phase. And in this section, I must admit I send some mixed signals because you need to find a balance between two seemingly disparate rules.

RULE 1: VALUE THE FOUNDATION
OF A LARGE BRAND

As an intrapreneur in the activation phase, you benefit from confidence in knowing you have a strong foundation behind you. You can walk the halls and take meetings with the knowledge that much of your strength derives from a source far bigger than your venture alone. If you're a team of two, externally you may project like a team of fifty. This can manifest in many ways. Think big and act with focus. Be ambitious in your communications, conveying your vision for success. Engage with vendors that have bigger reputations than your own. If you're a project within the halls of a big brand, it's likely that you can find capable vendors that would be eager to work with you—even if you are in the early activation phase. Consider creating a revenue-sharing option to help secure funding for your project. That's the sort of arrangement likely to get buzz in the halls.

Lisa West, a mobile marketing pioneer who helped a major hotel chain generate new income streams with mobile technology, describes this type of internal marketing and branding. "We had some big wins, and right away I said, 'Okay, let's share these publicly by applying for awards.' So, we applied for industry awards. And then those wins gave us even more validity because they were recognized externally." Then Lisa and her team took news of those industry awards and turned them back into a new internal marketing push. "We made sure that the right people internally within corporate comms, etcetera were aware." When you share good news internally—and add to that foundation to generate even more news—you build momentum for your project. It's the way you turn spectators into fans, Lisa says.[5]

Through these sorts of activities and tactics, you're helping others understand your success. You may still be some steps away from being truly material to the company's results, but you're acting and communicating your confidence that this will be so.

RULE 2: BE HUMBLE

And now for my possibly contradictory yet critically important advice: while you have grounds for confidence, you must, at the same time, retain your humility.

Humility can be a complicated concept. Don't rely on the dictionary alone; definitions range from a modest and respectful attitude toward oneself and others to a sense of unworthiness.

Instead, think of humility in its most basic form—a word that can come from the Latin *humilis*, translated as "humble or grounded," from the Latin word *humus,* translated as "earth." Take a position in your work that radiates this kind of humility—a sense of being grounded.

This does not suggest an air of being unworthy, and nor does it involve false humility. It does however demand that you not practice or project the polar opposite: arrogance.

Bill Burke has observed that in order to achieve success with intrapreneurship, it helps to be "someone people want to root for."[6] This is part of the softer side of making things work. By showing humility and care for others along with competence, you will make it a long way toward this goal.

Being arrogant—or even perceived as arrogant—will be a big derailer of an intrapreneur. You want to avoid that reputation. The arrogant intrapreneur provides detractors with an easy way to block the project. As I've said before, when you're an intrapreneur in a corporate enterprise, any number of forces can hinder you. If you develop a reputation for arrogance (and, aside from the substantive reasons specific to the situation, this is already a barrier to achieving full potential anyway), you've just given all those people a galvanizing force. Now, they don't have to convince anyone else about the value or efficacy of your project. Now, they can just say, "Oh, that person is so arrogant," and others will agree and sign on to the opposition. You made it easy.

High-profile entrepreneurs often have a different relationship with arrogance and humility. Self-confidence on steroids (which can easily migrate into arrogance) is a common feature for some successful entrepreneurs. It's not only an accepted behavior, but it can also be an expected behavior. While there are many humble entrepreneurs, you have to work harder to find them in some market sectors. The venture capital funding community often rewards the brash, swashbuckling innovator.

That's not the attitude that plays well in a corporate setting. Brash and swashbuckling will often get you negative attention. Self-confidence plays an important role, but self-promotion and arrogance cause multiple problems. So especially at the early activation stage of an intrapreneurial project, leaven your confidence and vision with humility, listening skills, and an understanding of organizational needs.

So, how do you put these two disparate pieces of guidance together? How can you be both humble and confident?

- **Consider your audience.** Different people will need different things from you. Your team or external partners may really need a higher level of visible confidence but the IT leader from whom you need resources may be more responsive to openly and genuinely expressed humility. Think about what your listener needs to see more of from you and adjust accordingly. Sometimes a subtle shift in emphasis works wonders—while always keeping your authenticity, your groundedness.

- **Consider your location.** You work for a big company, and you may have the opportunity to discuss your project within headquarters and out in the world. At a conference or other public space, you may be called upon to represent both your own project and the company's larger and presumably well-known brand. In that context, sharing the depth and breadth of your capabilities to help people makes sense. You are the face of the mothership brand at that moment. While maintaining humility, accuracy, and a customer focus, you also have the real opportunity to demonstrate the commitment your company has and the resources it is using to support the initiative. Make sure that you represent the full team, not just a portion of it. Back within your org walls, you are still the upstart in the mix. In the conference room, where everyone presumably knows the size and stage of your effort, consistently visible humility is a good rule.

- **Consider your team.** Much of what we've talked about revolves around how you will be perceived and judged by outside forces—your colleagues, your leaders, and your industry. But you must also consider what your team needs to hear at this stage of the project. This is the moment of activation. What do they need you to say and do in order to see that they've made a good choice to be part of this launch? And this will vary. Your team may need to hear a "we're going to land on the moon" speech. Or they may need to be reminded to think big but act humbly—the humble giant!—to move ahead but avoid unnecessarily negative attention from detractors.

Keith Wilmot offers this additional advice regarding humility: know when to let go. "The way I'd put it is to stay in your lane. As an intrapreneur, there's a time to be fully in and then there's a time to hand it over to an organization or a team of people that are really great at scale," he says. Intrapreneurs are often accomplished at developing a business in its early stages, but are not always the ones who will be the best choice to run a mature product. "They're really good at getting a concept and getting initiatives to a certain point. And then it often works best when at that point, they have the humility to take their hands off of it and allow others to bring it to scale."[7]

Said another way, while some people have the ability to migrate through the full arc of a business's development, many are much more naturally wired to excel at the different stages. Also, regardless of an intrapreneur's capabilities, some ventures can be sustained on their own over a long period of time, and others naturally fold into a preexisting business unit along the way.

On the topic of humility combined with an accurate understanding of the initiative's prospects, here's another facet an intrapreneur must consider: When do you discontinue the effort?

Some projects will never take off. Some will start and then flounder before they can grow strong roots. As an intrapreneur, you'll need to be able to spot the time when it's right to pull back or wind down the business or initiative. The question is: How do you know when—and how—to make that call?

Tom Daly saw that happen first-hand over two decades ago at another company. At the time, the advent of the web was creating many opportunities and many threats to existing businesses. An intrapreneurial project sprang up around this situation and went like this: by introducing a new online solution, they could help shape the emerging marketplace. Tom had big hopes for the effort. "It was an idea that was honed internally. We looked at outside experts to help develop that product and handle what was really a pretty technically heavy lift."[8]

But in the end, the project never took off. And when enthusiasm flagged internally, the team had to pull the plug. "I can't even tell you exactly why it didn't work. The product didn't do everything that we hoped. I'm not sure what anybody could have done differently. But it was a good effort, bright idea. Maybe the wrong time with the wrong tech or wrong messaging."

Sometimes an idea serves as a catalyst for important growth even when its original iteration does not materialize as planned.

A notable example of an intrapreneurial project that ultimately failed and yet provided tremendous benefits was Mobile ESPN. Mobile ESPN was a venture ESPN offered from November 2005 to December 2006, as a virtual wireless carrier service (also known as an MVNO in the industry: mobile virtual network operator). As Manish Jha, longtime ESPN senior executive and the general manager of this venture shared, "The investment that we made as a company in trying to build a mobile platform to serve sports fans on mobile devices, we didn't necessarily get the business model. But we learned so many things in that process, that ESPN since then and to this day has been one of the most successful businesses on the mobile platform in the world. And they wouldn't have done it, they couldn't have done it if they hadn't taken the risk and tried to figure it out early."[9]

I personally witnessed the arc of the Mobile ESPN business. Among other things, ESPN contracted with The Weather Channel to provide weather content for this service. We admired their commitment to investing in emerging platforms in the sports content category, which lends itself so naturally to mobile. Our team saw firsthand the tremendous benefits ESPN gained from an early commitment to mobile users, even if this particular initiative did not ultimately work as intended. We also learned more about how to build relationships with other content providers and wireless carriers for distribution of our weather on mobile devices, especially in coordination with other content types like sports. So, The Weather Channel's commitment to supporting this ESPN intrapreneurial venture ultimately helped us ascend the learning curve and grow our own business as well.

On Innovation Centers

Some large companies choose to establish innovation centers. These hubs provide a central resource for various people and company divisions to find allies for growth. They can operate on a "push" model by which they identify strategic opportunities for the company to pursue, and also a "pull" model by which they invite great ideas and provide an incubation center for them. Innovation centers, sometimes referred to as R&D Centers, have long been used with powerful effect, with many examples including iconic ones like Bell Labs. While much more has been written on this topic elsewhere, the people I spoke with on it expressed similar themes:

- Innovation centers should not be the only place where innovation happens in the company. Innovation can happen all around the company.

- Innovation centers need to pick a subset of the good ideas to focus on and prove value to the organization.

- These centers usually should not overly align with any one part of the broader business; rather, they should be a resource for any division that needs assistance, based on idea quality and organizational strategy.

- Innovation centers sometimes can generate ideas on their own. However, the majority of people I spoke with found ways to make new initiatives operational in coordination with existing and active business units. One key area to balance is actively engaging sizable business units on nascent and early initiatives, without allowing the existing operating business to squash them early on. These centers also typically rely on operating partners for insight and guidance.

- Active support from leaders around the company plays a central role in the effectiveness of the innovation center, including but not limited to the CEO.

Business activation in larger organizations can happen within an existing operating business, or in a center devoted to new growth. In either case, the early stages of activation include critical moments for your project. They must be handled carefully and yet with focus and commitment. Understanding how and where to direct your best efforts will give you the momentum you need to continue forward progress.

Chapter Summary

Entire books have been written about the activation of a new business. In this chapter, we review some key elements that are at a premium for an intrapreneur.

- Excel at core operational functions, including Product, Technology, Sales, and Marketing.

- Prove financial and strategic viability.

- Iterate.

- Serve your customers, team, and overall business as a humble explorer backed by a brand and resources.

- Learn from failure and apply these lessons.

- Where relevant, connect innovation centers with the broader organization, and allow them to serve as catalysts for strategic value creation.

CHAPTER 7

ENGAGE THE INDUSTRY

An intrapreneur operates within a larger organization. But that does not mean the intrapreneur lives in a cocoon. "Intrapreneur" does not mean all the work is done inside or that intrapreneurs can consider themselves some kind of corporate Lone Ranger.

Quite the opposite.

Intrapreneurs must make an even greater effort to reach out and make connections, both within their organizations and with a variety of entities beyond their own organizational walls.

If you are truly driving innovation with tangible results, then you have the opportunity to contribute in ways that matter not just to your company but also to the wider world. You may even be creating a new category. This means the work you do outside your corporate team may yield as much benefit to you and your marketplace as the work inside your walls. You're not just creating a new category—you're prepping the world to be ready for it.

Customers can't always articulate what they want. Companies can't indefinitely rely on existing methods to create and sell their offerings. To achieve more of their potential, they also have to create new models and lay the groundwork for their company's innovative new products and services.

We're not just talking about Oprah and Steve Jobs and Sara Blakely here. Intrapreneurs have long played an important role in this pathbreaking tradition as well. At times, the intrapreneur must prepare the industry to accept the innovative new product. This preparation means not only designing and launching a great offering but also engaging with the larger industry to accept and support it.

Since an intrapreneur doesn't usually go door-to-door to tout the benefits of a new product, they need to find different paths to get that message out.

We discuss the need to connect with expert talent from outside the organization in other chapters. We also cover the benefits of building relationships within your organization in order to secure support. In this chapter, we look more closely at an outside ecosystem that is tailor-made for the smart intrapreneur. We're talking about industry organizations, conferences and other professional events.

Too often, trade associations live in the background of the industry—they may not be as newsworthy or high-profile as the established corporate stars or the brash rising startups. They often can appear bureaucratic or slow to move due to the typical consensus required for major breakthroughs. Sure, if the organization hosts an annual planning or educational gathering in an exciting location, many people pay attention. Outside of that, though, they may forget to tap this resource.

This oversight is a mistake since in many industries, trade organizations become a critical foundational layer that enables participating entities to flourish. Industry organizations gather leaders to create the standards and frameworks that are needed to innovate. Industry organizations are where some of the most concentrated networking takes place, where boards find ways to balance the needs of various stakeholders, where new ideas bubble up for the first time in panels and presentations, and where ordinary hallway conversations can lead to the next great innovation. Industry organizations provide a forum for exploration and discussion that cross-pollinates new and old companies, allowing them to be creative in novel and successful ways.

Industry organizations play a particularly important role for intrapreneurs since they offer resources, support, and opportunities even before the mothership is fully committed to the new venture. Smart intrapreneurs can leverage their industry associations to supplement corporate support. They represent an important playing field for intrapreneurs for a variety of reasons.

Think through what your product needs right now and consider the possibilities of concentrated learning and discussions. How can you partner with your industry association? They offer a host of benefits.

Industry Orgs Are a Place to Seek Talent and Partners

You've come up with a big new idea that you're sure will be a winner. Internally, your company may give you initial support. Some key employees of the enterprise may believe in your initiative and offer some of their time and effort. But not everyone with a demanding schedule within your organization is going to be willing to ditch their day jobs and throw in with your experiment.

You may find a very different reception out in the broader industry.

As an intrapreneur backed by your larger entity, you often have elevated visibility at an industry event. Back at the home office, the intrapreneur may be a small player. Perhaps you have relatively little in the way of funding and revenue expectations. You're an internal experiment or early-stage business.

When you venture out into the industry association space, you carry the banner of your mothership brand. In some respects, you are as big and as high profile as any of your colleagues. You convene with others in similar situations. And that can work in your favor. For example, in the case of mobile media and marketing innovation, we gathered leaders from media companies, wireless carriers, technology enablers, and others who had aligned interests. We found our people.

Intrapreneurs will gather as much in the way of resources as possible from inside the firm. You can strengthen your efforts overall and complement internal capabilities by reaching out to others who would be delighted to partner with a brand the size and stature of yours—whether you have an early-stage internal startup or a sizable and fast-growing corporate business unit.

Industry associations are the perfect venue for the intrapreneur in search of knowledgeable experts and business partners. They tend to be a melting pot of the category, attracting a full range of interested people from beginners to industry veterans.

They include other businesses that may want to be partners with or vendors for your venture.

Some lucky intrapreneurs can find all the resources they need within their firms. Sometimes, a forward-thinking company will set up a quiet skunkworks inside its own walls. That project can grow and evolve until it's ready to burst with a fully realized initial offering out into the world.

But that's not the case for all intrapreneurs, and most will find themselves in the wider industry in search of business partners, talent, and support. Industry organizations can provide that resource.

Industry Orgs Are a Place to Meet Entrepreneurs

On a related note, industry organizations give intrapreneurs a way to connect with entrepreneurs in the space. This is often marketed as an opportunity for a new, brash upstart. Come to this organization and rub elbows with the elite leadership of your industry! And that's true. It's an entrée for the newcomer. But the value of this connection is not a one-way street.

When the intrapreneur and the entrepreneur meet, they have the opportunity to find ways to help each other. The entrepreneur may be looking for a way to gain visibility and market traction for an innovation. The intrapreneur may need someone with cutting-edge technical skills or innovative new products that aren't currently available in the larger corporate enterprise. I certainly had this experience at The Weather Channel.

I was active in the Mobile Marketing Association (MMA)

and got to know the team at a small company called Third Screen Media. They had aggressive growth plans but were not yet firmly established. They were a scrappy little startup with new software to serve mobile ads. Wanting to work with companies like The Weather Channel, they attended industry events so business observers would become aware of and engage with them.

A similar and reciprocal set of benefits applied to my team at The Weather Channel, as we were seeking to push the intrapreneurial mobile business forward. We could hold many productive discussions and learn rapidly about timely trends in a concentrated way.

While it was possible to set up standalone meetings in our offices, we often used industry conferences to bring larger groups of team members together cost-effectively, learn with other industry leaders together, and increase visibility for notable accomplishments. We sometimes built community more at broader events than smaller gatherings. The value of participation often appears clearest to the smaller firms, but the benefits of these forums accrue to larger ones too.

Industry Orgs Offer a Forum in Which to Advance Your Project—Globally

The nature of a successful intrapreneurial project is that it's new, it breaks new ground, it pushes boundaries, and it grows.

This very newness can block its advancement. Corporate leaders sometimes voice a desire to be cutting edge and first into the new horizon, but then balk when it's time to take that true leap forward. It's scary out there in the land of innovation. Plenty of senior executives hesitate when the landscape view ahead is too unclear.

For that reason, the industry association can be a true boon to the intrapreneur by providing guidance and standards that allow the innovative new idea to move forward with confidence.

I was part of this process in the early days of text messaging. When texting was new, there was a flurry of activity—and anxiety—over how to incorporate it into business strategy and revenue generation. Could the platform be useful for marketing? Would it be a meaningful channel for commercial advertising or to fundraise for worthy causes? Would companies adopt it? Would consumers accept it? Could a financial framework be established?

It was a time of great anticipation but also widespread confusion. Throughout the established telecom industry, there was a sense that we were all on the cusp of something big but also standing at the precipice of unique new dangers. Discussions within industry forums produced a lot of helpful insight on ways to chart the course and involved some painful decisions along the way.

To help us walk through a large portion of the needs, we gathered as an industry to develop consumer best practices (CBP) for SMS text messages and craft advertising guidelines for mobile websites and apps. We needed to use a high degree of discretion, especially in the emerging marketplace, in areas ranging from product selection to ad creative to technical challenges. In the process, we chose not to accept some large and otherwise attractive ad buys that violated our ad guidelines. However, we had developed industry and company standards to protect the user experience and our brand.

While continuing to drive innovation, we needed to retain confidence that our deals would fully follow our industry advertising guidelines, comply with government regulations, and remain within any other boundaries we set as a company.

And that's a great use case for an industry organization—to help create standards and generate insights so the industry has clear bearings informed by various stakeholders. Anything less risks missing some important aspect and making embarrassing, unnecessary missteps as a result.

To be sure, some government entities seek to regulate new businesses such as digital advertising. And they do! But the smart businesses will get ahead of that government effort (which can take years) and engage an industry association to draft guidelines where relevant.

Pascal Racheneur remembers these early days of mobile. It was a time when new companies and industry associations were all trying to figure out the best way forward. To make decisions that would give the industry security, he observed we needed "evangelist" leadership that could step into the forefront.[1] We were both involved in it.

We joined a team of over fifty people sponsored by the MMA tasked with creating a text messaging code of conduct. Fifty is a ridiculously large number for a committee—but that large a group was necessary. We were moving into uncharted territory, and the full communications industry had to be involved. We heard from many parties and got agreement across different industry segments for this to be successful. We had a very large group of people, and each had an imprint on the results.

I recall our gatherings in huge conference rooms as we hashed out the issues. I also recall our after-work outings and one memorable trip to see a rodeo in Denver. It seemed like a natural reflection of our work to watch cowgirls and cowboys attempting to rope errant steers and ride bucking horses. Our efforts around text messaging also felt very pioneering at the time. But it was that group, under the auspices of the MMA in this case, that allowed us as industry leaders to create a roadmap for advertising on our shared new mobile platform.

By participating in and supporting our industry associations, we were able to move our own intrapreneurial efforts forward. With guidelines, I was in a better position to say yes the next time a potential advertiser wanted to write us a big check. Guidelines allow a deal like that to happen while enabling new revenue streams and minimizing the risk of ending up on the front page of the *Wall Street Journal*, criticized for having too few protections for consumers.

Industry Organizations Are a Great Team Management Tool

As an intrapreneur, you see your team working hard every day. You see them risking the comfort and stability of a regular corporate assignment to go out on a limb with you. You see them putting their own personal reputations on the line to throw in with your idea. You want to give them everything in return—but your budget is limited by the scope of your project.

An industry organization can help you find mutually beneficial development opportunities for your team members.

Intrapreneurs often work in the shadows amid larger groups of people. Industry organizations offer many opportunities to volunteer—to participate on a committee, to lead an outreach effort, or to serve in organizational leadership roles. The industry organization needs this type of participant to function, much less excel. Those who put their time and effort in can also reap rewards. This is a way to learn, contribute, and raise your profile in the industry. Particularly when you are employed by a large company, volunteering in a leadership role can give you a chance to have a broader impact.

As the leader of an intrapreneurial project, this is an opportunity for you to encourage your team members to step into the spotlight, too. You can—and often should—encourage them to participate and contribute. As a team leader, you're in a position to manage the time commitment and travel budget. When you do this, the positive results are many. You raise the profile of your project by sending a team member into a more visible role with the industry association. This generates positive buzz around your innovation effort. It's also a way to provide recognition and a reputation boost to your team members. You may not have access to all the resources they would prefer in the early days of a nascent effort, but you can help them become more experienced and active in the industry.

Industry awards offer a great chance to recognize important work by intrapreneurial teams. Many companies give awards annually and provide a moment to shine in the spotlight. Internal corporate awards are great, and broader internal recognition supported by great performance conveys many benefits. That said, it's quite another thing for the team to win awards like an Emmy or a Peabody or other industry awards for excellence. When you encourage your team members to volunteer for industry organization roles, you give them a chance to boost their morale, enhance their reputations, and strengthen their loyalty to your team. I remember the leaders who encouraged me to step into the spotlight. It's a vote of confidence that sticks with you over the years.

Industry Associations Provide Valuable Learning Opportunities

Industry conventions and meetings are designed as learning opportunities. Many even sort their content into particular learning tracks so attendees can customize their visits and learn on topics of highest interest to them.

But many of the most impactful benefits occur outside of the scripted content. Here are a few of them:

- **Learn about emerging trends.** When you're watching a panel discussion or listening to the Q&A after a keynote, you can hear more about known trends. You can also pick up on what's not being said expressly—such as the fault lines that may be emerging in the industry. When you hear disagreements or see conflicting evidence, you can discern better what will happen next in those areas.

- **Learn who to engage professionally (and possibly hire) and who to be more careful about.** Industry events expose you to the types of people who may not yet be accessible through the traditional channels of a larger firm. This is where you can meet entrepreneurs and other independent talent. It also allows you to connect with employees of other big firms. These may be individuals representing organizations that you want to establish or expand a business relationship with going forward.

- **Dive beneath the surface, the headlines, and the press releases.** Hallway conversations in industry events present great opportunities to pick up on milestones, insights, and trends. Discretion is necessary, especially in a big company. When you're a one-person startup, you can go around saying a lot of whatever you like. When you work within the walls of a corporate hierarchy, you're expected to keep confidential information confidential. At the same time, a lot of things are clearly shareable and valuable; they just require you to show up and participate. When you have enough discussions of this sort, you can make better decisions.

- **Build trust with others while protecting sensitive information.** On that last point about confidentiality, some people are too lax. Please go back to your basic principles. With public company information, people must be careful in some very specific ways by law and regulation. With private company information, much is still confidential and more is in the gray zone. Use discretion. I've long tried to ask myself a question that others have suggested to me in the past: If this were reported on the front page of a prominent website or newspaper, how would I feel about it? If the answer is fully positive, it's probably ok to share. If not, be very careful. If in doubt, protect the interests of all involved by not sharing. If you follow this guidance, you will learn more of the things that can reasonably be shared while also showing you can be trusted, too.

In Case Things Don't Work

There's another reason to be active as an intrapreneur in an industry organization. No matter how confident you are, no matter how skilled your team is, and no matter how innovative and robust your initiative may be, it can still go sideways or down the drain.

As an intrapreneur, you're taking a risk. There are many safer ways to make one's way through the corporate journey. When you push the boundaries of an organization, you're making it clear that you think something new and different should be embraced by the firm.

You may be 100 percent right, and if it all goes according to plan, everyone is more successful for it. Or maybe not. It's unusual for a venture to proceed fully according to the original plan.

Sometimes, despite your best efforts, an intrapreneurial project hits a wall. It may simply fade and sputter out. Or it may crash and burn in spectacular fashion. Sometimes, that's due to a fault in the idea or implementation, but many times it's the result of outside forces: the technology changes, a new leadership team is installed, a change in the customer landscape demands new tactics, a downturn in your broader industry necessitates layoffs and other cutbacks, or your boss and primary provider of resources and air cover leaves and takes a new job. All these things can affect your project.

Sometimes, a failed project is accepted and everyone moves on, ideally with a lot of valuable learning. But sometimes, a role changes so much that one must change too. Not only might you be in the position of looking for a different role, but also other first-rate people may be in similar situations—and you may be able to help them find a new opportunity that is a perfect fit.

For these reasons, an intrapreneur is wise to have a network. Even if you're not job hunting, it's preferable to have a range of strong relationships. This is certainly true for intrapreneurs, who are taking a somewhat riskier path than some of their corporate colleagues. Industry associations are obvious ways to maintain connections and expand perspective.

Making the Right Association Choice— and Investment

Industry associations have paid staff, and they also rely on the enthusiastic participation of volunteers to thrive. They are like magnets, often pulling you in closer. They can also have a wide range of needs over time—more money, more time, more energy.

We detail the important ways an industry association can benefit an intrapreneur, but still, it's important to keep one's own goals and priorities in focus. Industry associations often want more from you. As a participant, you need to make your own calculation as to what level of investment makes sense and when and how to put those hours to good use.

Here are some questions to ask yourself:

WHICH ASSOCIATIONS SHOULD I PRIORITIZE?

For many in large industries, this question deserves some careful thought. Vibrant sectors of the economy typically offer multiple association opportunities. You may find a major legacy trade association, a scrappy upstart group, one that focuses on domestic representation, another that is global in its focus—the list goes on. The bigger the industry, the more likely it is to have a range of groups to choose from.

You can keep them all on your dashboard, but your time and resources are still limited. You'll need to make choices about which ones will be most valuable to your project, your team, and you personally.

To apply a useful litmus test, go back to the core statements for your project. Which individual association (or group of them) most supports your vision, goals, and values? The answer to this question will be a good indication about how to participate at this juncture. If the project requires industry development including standards and policy, an association committed to meeting these needs has high potential. If your team requires technical development, then an association focused more on engineering needs may be more compelling. Understand the goals of the industry organizations and match them with your own as appropriate.

HOW MUCH TIME CAN I DEVOTE TO AN ASSOCIATION?

I'll say again: the ambitious and effective industry association often will take as much time as you allow. This is particularly true once you've successfully shown leadership and commitment on an association project. You'll be tapped time and again. This can be of tremendous value to you and to your project, so it's a good thing, generally speaking. But it's possible to over-index on industry organization work.

It can siphon time from your team and your project. Remember that your own intrapreneurial work must come first over time. If your team can't find you on a regular basis when needed due to your outside commitments or if you're distracted by peripheral requests and you're not giving your in-house demands your first energy, that's when the association work has gone too far. You need to be aware of the amount of time you have to give to an outside organization—and stick to that boundary. Sometimes a major project, role, or event requires focus for a distinct period of time. If so, meet that need and then revert to a more normal time allocation. Of course, ideally, your business needs and association participation have so much in common that this will not be an issue. Regardless, your first priority must be your team.

Association commitments can drain your energy. No matter how much stamina you have—and intrapreneurs are often very energetic people—you have limits. You need to understand where to draw the line. This is not simply a question of making time for your team; you must also consider your personal priorities. Even when you're committed to working hard, it's fundamentally important to remember non-professional needs and interests like health, family, friends, and hobbies. The average industry organization won't tell you to do that; you need to carve that time out yourself and communicate your participation abilities. Industry organizations don't have quality of life coordinators who will step up to guide you with that. It's your job.

Ultimately, industry associations allow you to reach beyond your walls to make connections, build relationships, learn, grow, contribute, and thrive. For the intrapreneur, these collective benefits provide great value, and in some cases, one that yields breakthrough opportunities in the course of building your business and developing your career.

Chapter Summary

Here we review the ways industry associations can be a key success factor for an intrapreneur.

- Develop knowledge through participation in industry organizations and events.

- Expand your network and build stronger relationships by sharing a forum with a wide range of experts and potential business partners, including entrepreneurs with cutting-edge technology and capabilities.

- Advance your industry through your and your company's participation, building a stronger ecosystem for all.

- Give team members opportunities to grow and contribute through participation in associations and events, including leadership roles.

- Distribute industry responsibilities and opportunities thoughtfully among team members.

- Use discretion with the number of organizations you participate in and your total time commitment to achieve a reasonable balance over time.

CHAPTER 8

GIVE BACK

When is it time to give back? When you've reached a certain executive level? When your company has arrived at a certain size or stature? When you have more time?

I'd advocate turning that question on its head—when *isn't* it a good time to give back?

Intrapreneurs can feel like small fish in a big pond. And in the most literal sense, that's true. In terms of physical or financial size, the intrapreneurial team can be the pipsqueak in any large organization. I've been on intrapreneurial teams that weren't big enough to field a good softball team at the company picnic.

But when it comes to the concept of giving back to the community, intrapreneurs should not feel as if they are too small to make a difference. In fact, they can have an impact that belies their actual size in the marketplace.

What's more, intrapreneurs have a unique responsibility when it comes to giving back to the community. Intrapreneurs often represent what's next in large organizations. How intra-preneurs behave and how they act around commitments related to "giving back" will be noted. Those watching see this as an example of what they can expect, not just from this one new business but from the company overall. Intrapreneurs set a vis-ible example of organizational behavior.

At the same time, intrapreneurs must sometimes make an extra effort in this area. When we work for a large company on the organization's broad overall mission, it's easy to mentally outsource the role of giving back to others. The bigger the parent organization, the more likely it is there's a person or even a full department devoted to community engagement. As an individ-ual fish in a very big pond, you can probably show up a couple of times a year for community events that your colleagues organize. You can be part of a fundraiser, clean up a playground, or speak at a school function and you will have done your part.

The intrapreneur plays a different role at times. Certainly, the intrapreneur is still a company employee and can participate in activities related to giving back that are organized on the broader corporate level. You can both participate in the overall activities and also select ways to give back that relate to the interests of the immediate intrapreneurial team.

That is precisely why the intrapreneur should step up. In a tiny team (where it sometimes seems that everyone is doing three jobs, is under-resourced for time and money, and is feeling heavy pressure to deliver), the heat is on. If giving back is important to the team, then the intrapreneur must lead by example. People notice both your talk and your walk. In these early days, you set the tone and the spirit for what your new project will be in the world. Giving back is not just a process of giving time or money. It's about how you show up in the world. And how an intrapreneur acts in this area sends a valuable signal, just as the way a CEO shows up sends a clear message too. The difference is primarily a question of scale.

Philip Nutsugah, longtime product leadership executive at companies including Cox Communications and Verizon, sums it up this way: "The world is bigger than any of us. That ground-edness puts what you do at work into perspective."[1] When you engage with the community around you, he noted, you gain a sense of fulfillment as well as lessons that can be applied in work and in life. "The better person you are, the better employee or the better leader you are."

In this chapter, we look at ways the intrapreneur can give back to the community—not just as an individual but also as a team. It can be tempting to keep one's head down and focus on the project, letting others take care of the charitable giving. But if your project is worthy of scale, it's worthy of a place in the community. You can start strong by establishing a commitment to a habit of giving back from the project's opening days.

Keep this mantra in your head for guidance: show up.

Show Up for Your Community— No Matter What You Do

Some businesses are more visibly well-suited to community con-tributions than others. The corporate mandate seems to exude a higher mission. I know I felt that when I worked at The Weather Channel and at CNN. Whatever else I was doing on any given day, I felt connected to the mission. Whatever task might be on my desk, I was part of the larger effort to keep people safe and informed about the weather affecting them or explain the world to viewers through our unique global newsgathering capabilities. When we did a good job at these things, our customers knew more about important events in a way that might not be part of their conversations otherwise.

Some companies won't have a similar obvious mission with purpose. Some employers appear to be much more focused on simply making money as priorities one, two, and three. And while profitability is important and necessary, I've always seen it as insufficient. These types of assignments alone seem to lack that higher purpose.

But those other firms actually didn't lack a higher purpose most of the time. My feeling of insignificance was actually my own failure of imagination. A business can play a positive role in the marketplace even when its mission may appear largely financial. The dealership that sells cars may only seem to be selling cars, but that action could create a positive economic ripple effect through the community. So too, a factory, a financial firm, or a technology enterprise—when they do well—can spin off that wealth. Their leaders move into the community and serve on the boards of hospitals and museums and Boys & Girls Clubs. Their success makes a community stronger. It's up to those within the walls to imagine what's possible. I had to learn that truth.

Here's an example from my own work. I served as an

intrapreneur with the Cox Media division of Cox Communications and wanted to understand better how to give back. We were not a general news organization, a nonprofit, or The Weather Channel, warning people to take shelter to survive a coming storm. We provided a cross-platform advertising portfolio for a cable company. We helped a lot of people, and yet the broader contributions sometimes hid behind the marketing campaigns and financial transactions.

Then COVID-19 hit.

In general, everybody's business fell off a cliff. We could see it all around us. Traditional advertisers shut down their spending. Office buildings shut down their locations. Everything seemed to retreat into closed spaces, and businesses that relied on in-person communities experienced an immediate impact.

As an intrapreneurial team, we could see at least two things: our communities were in need from coast to coast and we had a whole lot of available ad space. So, our team came up with a way to put those two things together.

We began to offer our ad space—available ad units that we would have earmarked for big media buys—to local businesses, most of which were restaurants. We ran something like $3 million worth of ads. We knew there might be a bit of goodwill around this, but mostly we thought it would help our neighbor community businesses get by during a crisis.

We underestimated the impact in multiple ways. Not only was this a huge boon to local businesses, but also the goodwill it generated for the company was enormous. Our team was surprised and gratified by this reaction. We heard about it over and over. We had acted to help our community. And in doing so, our team reinforced our genuine longstanding commitment to the communities we serve.

I think about that example often when I'm talking with intrapreneurs. I remind them that it's not always obvious how you can help or what the impact of the effort will be. But sometimes giving back means stepping up in a moment that is unpredicted—such as in a pandemic.

Support the Intrapreneurs within Nonprofits

John Hancock, a longtime leader in the Junior Achievement network, observes that "we stay more relevant if there's intrapreneurship."[2] To support this point, he describes a breakthrough concept with JA BizTown, a program that now stands as a hallmark offering within the Junior Achievement suite of student programs and experiences. The breakthrough came in the mid-1990s when the organization's Indianapolis chapter formed a partnership with a Kansas City–based nonprofit organization called The Learning Exchange. The Learning Exchange had been established by a group of former teachers interested in promoting the importance and effectiveness of experiential education. Among other initiatives, The Learning Exchange developed Exchange City (the precursor to JA BizTown). Junior Achievement had long been a leader in experiential learning models but saw an opportunity to get even better. What began as a simple licensing arrangement eventually resulted in Junior Achievement purchasing the rights to revise and replicate JA BizTown. Nearly thirty years later, JA BizTown has spread to more than thirty-five markets around the country, and a sequel program called JA Finance Park has been created to complement the learning in JA BizTown.

So, when looking for ways to give back, you have an opportunity to benefit the nonprofit organizations you care about not only through donations but also through support for the innovators within these organizations, including with strategic insights from your own experiences and partnership for growth.

Show Up for Education—at All Levels

There is a unique mandate for the intrapreneur when it comes to education. Your team is engaged in something that is cutting-edge and new to everyone—even to your executive team! You are an educator all the time within your own enterprise walls, explaining to everyone why your project will be successful and worthwhile. Look for ways to extend that educator mode outside of your own team and into the community. There are many ways, large and small, that you can engage in education there.

You can take on a big project and agree to be a partner for a school. As an example, our team supported Junior Achievement and its 3DE program, which "re-engineers high school education to be more relevant, experiential, and authentically connected to the complexities of the real world."[3] These programs engage closely with the school to create powerful, life-changing outcomes for many of the participating students.

That's a major initiative with broad impact—one of many. In fact, Junior Achievement itself has practiced intrapreneurship for over a century as a nonprofit organization and generated profound benefits in the process. It has delivered so much impact globally that it was nominated for a Nobel Peace Prize.

Another way to educate is to offer internships. Your team may be small but that often means you can use some additional people power. An intern can engage in a meaningful, ongoing way. I have seen interns who went on to work for their companies with great success. An internship can be a small effort—simply a spot on your team for a few weeks. Or it can be more expansive and a partnership with other organizations in the community. But the experience provides valuable life lessons and new perspectives for the students who travel the internship road. This learning takes place in a real business in a way that is difficult to replicate in a classroom.

But don't assume that all education demands a classroom or a young student. As I worked through my own intrapreneurial efforts, I often thought, "I wish someone had told me about this beforehand." This happened routinely, most especially in my earliest intrapreneurial projects.

It's why I'm writing this book, to contribute to the education of the next generation of intrapreneurs on the process of innovating within the walls of a larger enterprise.

Sharing your own knowledge is the sort of contribution that any intrapreneur can make. Whether you hold seminars, arrange brown bag lunches, or mentor someone who wants to learn the process, you can share what you know about being an intrapreneur and give back via education. You don't need the framework of a school or a program. You can make it happen on your own terms. Commit to being an educator with your own cohort— the intrapreneurs.

Show Up for Your Team and Who They Are Meant to Be

When you give back to a community, you're not just supporting people who live in a town, city, or region. You can give back to a community that is defined differently—such as your team.

It may seem strange for a moment to consider your coworkers your community. When using that term, we are often referring to people outside the (literal or figurative) office walls. But your team is another type of community, one that you interact with closely. These are the people who are part of your professional ecosystem. They are connected to you, and they can be highly impacted by what you do and say. As part of giving back to your community, don't forget this nearby group. One of the things you can do to give back here is to help your teammates be whoever it is they are meant to be.

It's a big concept and one that we don't always address in day-to-day work life. We are on a trajectory that will take us on a journey through roles, experiences, or both. And eventually, if we're lucky, to a full expression of who we can be. The people you work with today are on that journey—with a mix of individual goals and possibilities. Give back to them by working with them to understand who they can and want to be and how you can help them move toward that potential.

As Brené Brown observes in her book *Dare to Lead*, "I define a leader as anyone who takes responsibility for finding the potential in people and processes, and who has the courage to develop that potential."[4] Picking up on Brown's insight, helping people and improving the way things are done are truly core aspects of being a successful leader. In turn, they apply inherently to intrapreneurs. While these contributions do not always come quickly or easily, they make a big difference and help us develop more of our own potential at the same time that we help others grow.

While using reasonable discretion, this means establishing a habit of consistently looking for ways to lift up your teammates. It's not always how we're trained as managers. When we rise in leadership roles, it's often because we can see what the company needs and then we engage the people within our walls to make that happen.

When we show up for this first layer of our community, we swap out the order of operations. We think: What does this individual need to achieve their goals?

In the context of a corporate role, you have ongoing and well-established responsibilities for stewardship of the organization. As part of doing the right thing, you should always practice those. However, assuming the basic requirements of these responsibilities are met, in the context of coaching team members, I've found that it's generally preferable to think about the person first. This has some meaningful implications, such as when a team member comes to you looking for career guidance and perspective. In general, I try to think of what will help them succeed the most first and then how our organization can help them second.

Often, with some luck and imagination, you can make both goals happen at the same time—serving the individual and the company. If one of your best product managers shows up in your office and says that they really want to pursue a career in business development, you can look for ways to intertwine the options. The product manager can continue product managing while you make sure they get additional business development assignments.

You can help that individual to grow, develop, and move toward their professional goals. That may work out for the company. You may be training your next superstar business development leader! Or perhaps you are giving this person enough exposure to the business development field to realize that, in fact, product management is where they're meant to be after all.

So many managers won't do this, due to a variety of concerns including a loss of short-term productivity and potential fear that the newly trained individual will leave and go to work elsewhere. These things may happen. But if so, that's not necessarily a net loss to you. You showed up for that individual and helped that person achieve a goal. Chances are good that person will be more fulfilled doing what they most want to do. Possibly they'll model your support for them and help other people to explore more of their own potential in the future, too. And while this isn't the motivation or expectation, perhaps they will look for ways to support your team in the future, even if it's from another position. We remember the people who show up for us. We know they gave us something and considered us a worthy member of their community. We are open to sustaining that relationship and appreciate the opportunity to pay it forward in other ways. This creates a virtuous circle. Maybe the goodness doesn't come back to you, but it does to someone else—the way you certainly have been helped by others in a selfless manner along the way.

Many successful intrapreneurs will tell you it was their early experiences and the support of their own intrapreneurial team leaders that put them on the path to success. For that reason, intrapreneurs should consider their work as the training of the next generation of leadership. It may be for their current company. It may be for another organization. But when intra-preneurs take on ambitious team members, they are giving back to their community by ensuring the next generation has the training and early experiences to do well over time.

Lesley Wainwright, longtime business and legal leader in the media industry, sees this in her own career and those around her. Intrapreneurs are developing their own capabilities and prepar-ing for expanded responsibilities in the future.

The projects themselves may be relatively modest, but the impact over time is not. She says, "Oftentimes, it doesn't really make that big of a dent in the bottom line for the overall enter-prise, but for that individual, they get to cut their teeth really early on. . . . You can't grow any better as a leader than actually getting to have a test case, almost a petri dish of leadership."

She goes on: "I'm a product of intrapreneurship and a prod-uct of different leaders at various points who invested in me."

Leading internal projects allowed her to explore and learn from within the company:

> In a lot of different ways, it allowed me to perform as an executive leader well before I was really ready for it. And so, by the time that the opportunity came for me to take on still broader executive responsibilities, I'd already been building those skills in real-life settings for many years.
>
> It's usually a really small team that is put on one of these initiatives. For the team and project to thrive, you have to expand beyond your obvious skill set. So, in many of those instances, I was the lawyer, but I was also on the executive or leadership team. We would sit around

the table, and we would ideate about the strategic direction of the business or project. And yes, I often would do that through the legal lens.

But at the same time, I started building and flexing these new leadership, collaboration, and strategy muscles. For example, I had to dive into the budget and spend time with the finance and product teams to be able to understand the business and contribute. So, long before I was actually responsible for my own budget items, teams, and operations, I was able to fully observe and learn through these experiences.

And that's what these opportunities do—they prepare team members to be more strategically minded leaders, and they often inspire those leaders to find and build similar opportunities for future generations. So, whether you go off on your own entrepreneurial path, or whether you stay and grow and use that skill set within the organization, this experience benefits you personally, benefits the organization, and benefits the industry at large.

When you train the next generation, as intrapreneurial teams do, you give a gift to the future.[5]

Too often, I find people believe that giving back is somehow a task for a date and time far into the future. Some people even want to wait until they retire before doing community activities. When this point of view comes up, as a rule, I encourage them to consider getting involved now. I strongly disagree that community involvement should wait until you have excess free time. I think it's important to engage in the community in an ongoing way as practical, admittedly with some flexing based on individual circumstances.

Of course, everyone makes decisions based on the totality of needs in their life, and this means some people have sound reasons to hold back from additional commitments. That said, from my perspective, most intrapreneurs should NOT wait to retire (or even to just have a lot more flexible time) before they get involved in giving back to the community in some way that is positive and floats that person's boat. I think they should do it NOW. And rotate through activities over time as sensible and practical.

Ultimately the process of giving back is one that demands that the intrapreneur understand what community really means. It means more than the standard definition of community—those who live and work in the physical neighborhoods adjacent to our offices or share a common interest. It also encompasses the young people not yet in the workforce, the colleagues we see day in and day out, and those who would travel intrapreneurial roads alongside us one day. All of these people are members of our community. And all can benefit from attention and support.

Chapter Summary

Too often, people in smaller divisions of an organization think the role of "giving back" applies more to people in other, larger areas. In this chapter, we dispense with that misconception and show the ways an intrapreneur can be a supportive part of the larger community.

- Build giving back into your overall approach from early on.

- Set an example by finding ways to apply your team's unique strengths to addressing community needs.

- Expand your own perspective and knowledge through active participation in community activities.

- When you have a limited budget, find low-cost, high-impact volunteer options.

- Provide assignments, offer training, and serve as a mentor for other team members, especially ones with high potential to serve as next-generation intrapreneurial leaders.

- Overall, make a commitment to ensuring that your team, company, community, and beyond are better places thanks to your contributions and dedication.

WHY THE WORLD NEEDS INTRAPRENEURS. LOTS OF THEM.

Here we come to the end of our exploration for now, and I leave you with some important insights that emerged from this writing project with striking clarity.

Throughout this book, we highlight ways that intrapreneurship benefits the broader organization. We also identify how it increases effectiveness and fulfillment for individuals and teams. We even venture into how it contributes foundational positive change within an industry.

Overall, a broad observation emerged from my experience and interviews: *intrapreneurship makes the world a better place.* And we need more of it. Intrapreneurs are uniquely suited to act as catalysts for positive, profitable, and necessary developments in the world's economy.

Here are some important reasons why.

1. Intrapreneurs Push Established Organizations to Adapt

The world is full of established organizations that drive large portions of the world economy. These are institutions that employ hundreds, thousands, and even hundreds of thousands of people. They take many forms, including service providers, manufacturers, financial institutions, technology leaders, communications stalwarts, media companies, and so many more. They are established companies of various sizes. They play a vital role in creating prosperity for a large portion of people around the world.

But many corporations can become insular, cut off from the innovations around them. This lack of change allows a company to atrophy from the inside. Think about giants of bygone eras like Kodak, Blockbuster, Sears, Pan Am, and BlackBerry. There was a time when few in the areas they served could imagine the world without these brands. Yet, today, MBA programs share their stories as cautionary tales. They all suffered from the same disease: a failure to adapt successfully.

Intrapreneurs bring the cure to that ailment. Intrapreneurs bring the skill set that fits exceptionally well with the reality of continuous change. For companies so big and successful today that they shy away from outside help, intrapreneurs are the voice of change, creativity, and innovation. They are the insiders with the outsider perspective. They are positioned to help a big company see the possibilities and embrace the future.

It's one thing for a strong company to stay relevant in a current market or with a specific customer base. It's another to take a winning approach and expand it into other areas, making the organization stronger while also providing more solutions for customers, and strengthening communities in the process.

2. Intrapreneurs Train the Next Generation of Leaders

Read a leader's biography and you'll often find their origin story—the moment at which an individual could see forward and imagine themselves in a leadership role, taking an initiative or company in a bold new direction. That story can emerge in an entrepreneurial space, to be sure. At a large scale around the world, intrapreneurs also expand this training ground and give it a platform within many of the world's biggest and most innovative companies.

Even as employees serve the current mission of an organization, they can imagine and experience how to contribute in new and innovative ways. Intrapreneurs can then create those experiences for themselves and for their teams. This is the way many new leaders emerge from within the ranks of an enterprise, not walled off from the change around them but trained to face it and embrace it.

Any large enterprise should ask itself: How well do we practice the kind of training and empowerment that will surface our next generation of leadership? And how high is our comfort level with trying the new and untested in search of innovation? Do we celebrate and apply the learning from all these experiences, not just the successes?

If the enterprise doesn't offer an environment with growth opportunities, exploration, and risk tolerance, why should promising talent stay? Intrapreneurship provides the early experiences that will appear in the next generation of leadership biographies.

3. Intrapreneurs Create Transformative Growth Opportunities for Entrepreneurs

Imagine the hot, up-and-coming entrepreneur with an innovative new product or service. Once they get the first version of their product or service ready for the marketplace, what's their next move?

Obviously, the final destination is worldwide admiration. Well, maybe that's rarer than it appears. However, it's a dream for many entrepreneurs. But there's an interim step and that's the one I want to focus on here. At some point, the entrepreneur will want to take things up a notch. And often, that means partnering with an established enterprise. That's where intrapreneurs come in. Within the walls of a large enterprise, it's often the intrapreneur that is trying to do something new and different. The intrapreneur and the entrepreneur often have reciprocal, compatible, mirror-image needs. So, the intrapreneur can be the individual who will be most open to the entrepreneur's pitch.

This is the person who can create an entry point for someone who has just invented something entirely new and is looking for a path to wider adoption.

Intrapreneurs can be the entrepreneur's best friend. Do big organizations sometimes feel impersonal, large, and slow to move? Yes, and it is important to take this possibility into account. When you find an entrepreneurial solution that truly meets a critical need and a company that practices intrapreneurial excellence, the magic can happen. Consider all the new and promising ideas incubating in small companies all over the world. Intrapreneurs can give those ideas entry into the robust framework of an established enterprise.

4. Intrapreneurs Drive Value Creation Within the Organization

Intrapreneurs drive new growth opportunities within established organizations. As home improvement and airline industry expert Sterling Gerdes summarizes, "Most of the new value is created through intrapreneurship."[1]

Intrapreneurs also accelerate growth. As global marketing leader and respected author Janet Balis observes, "Intrapreneurship is one of the fastest paths to value creation."[2]

Overall, intrapreneurs lead a large portion of the most meaningful new growth within larger enterprises. They also have the ability to effect these advances at a rapid clip, especially after an initiative has passed its start-up stages. It's like a transformative lever that already exists within the capabilities of the organization, available to any person and team that successfully identifies attractive opportunities and then harnesses their potential.

In the process of creating and accelerating value within an organization, intrapreneurs have the opportunity not only to build but also to practice values that stand the test of time. When effective and team-oriented, they serve as role models for others to emulate. I see at least three primary behaviors that span multiple disciplines, infusing intrapreneurial initiatives with particular sustaining strength. The first is to hold fast to your principles, even in the middle of the storm. The second is to show up for your team. And the third is to combine curiosity with excellent listening skills to harness the full potential of your initiatives.

I want to leave you with this message: *intrapreneurs serve as the critical catalyst in global innovation.* They often don't get the same attention as entrepreneurs, venture capitalists, and other creativity generators. Some of these other impressive people are the players you see featured in the news, honored at industry conventions, and giving the keynotes. But intrapreneurs are an integral part of that ecosystem. They do their work within the walls of strong, established entities to make innovation, change, and creativity possible. Intrapreneurs help big organizations find their agile, inner spark.

And the world needs more of them. Lots more.

ACKNOWLEDGMENTS

No book is an island and I have many people to thank.

I'd like to start by expressing appreciation to the people who contributed to this writing journey by sharing thoughts during interviews on intrapreneurship: Ashlee Adams, Decker Anstrom, Michael Britt, Bill Burke, Doug Busk, Tom Daly, Loretta Daniels, Jim DiAndreth, Joe Fiveash, Rusty Friddell, Sterling Gerdes, John Hancock, Paul Iaffaldano, Manish Jha, Quincy Johnson, Craig Kirkland, Katie Klein, Juan Andrés Muñoz, Philip Nutsugah, Aidoo Osei, Jason Pastras, Marie Quintero-Johnson, Pascal Racheneur, Vicki Raimey, Scot Safon, Lee Scoggins, Elizabeth Snively, Joshua Sommer, Quint Studer, Jim Trupiano, Derek Van Nostran, Lesley Wainwright, Lisa West, Keith Wilmot, and Debora Wilson. Thank you to others, including Janet Balis, Bahns Stanley, and Chris Walters, who also contributed time and insights related to the book. You have all taken this concept and helped it to come to life. The original idea to conduct interviews to benefit readers has turned into so much more than just a few resulting insights—these discussions have enriched my understanding and the content of the book, start to finish.

Thank you to many people in the wider business community for advising me along the way. In particular, I appreciate the observations of Quint Studer and Dottie DeHart, who helped me with early guidance on the book. Thanks to Angelique Bellmer-Krembs, Tim Elmore, Andrew Feiler, Randy Hain, Arthur Klebanoff, Matt Holt, Chrissa Pagitsas, Tom Smallhorn, Josh Smith, Marty Speight, and Judy Train, who helped me with impactful assistance. Thank you to the team that convened to shape the questions for this book and vet the approach, including Craig Kirkland, Lisa West, Pascal Racheneur, and Derek Van Nostran. I extend profound appreciation to some especially amazing mentors and friends including Jill Campbell, Lisa Chang, Joe Fiveash, Susan Grant, Steve Hassett, Alec Horniman, Paul Iaffaldano, Sandhi Kozsuch, Lem Lewis, John Lowe, Wonya Lucas, Jim Manis, Jay McDonald, Eric Olson, Dave Scott, Bahns Stanley, Jody Stewart, Jing Wang, John Yates, and many more. You mean so much to me and this book would not be what it is without you.

To the countless people with whom I have worked, built community organizations, studied, traded reading recommendations, and shared adventures, I salute you here. Also, to the other leaders who have created environments conducive to the intrapreneurial success that our teams have enjoyed, I express appreciation and admiration. I know that numerous other people could be included here specifically, and please excuse any omissions. The butterfly effect is alive and well and it's sometimes hard to tell where one conversation ends and another begins. To the extent that this book offers benefit and insight, please consider yourself part of the experiences that shaped it.

While the career journey has generated lots of insight and learning, none for me surpasses the foundational growth at The Weather Channel. I want to express particular gratitude to a wide range of talented and committed people—teammates, business partners, and explorers—for eight great years of innovation and value creation as we continued the tradition of excellence with one of the most trusted brands in the world.

Thank you to my editorial and publishing team. To the amazing Ellen Neuborne, you are truly world-class. As my writing coach, editor, and expert on a wide range of things related to communicating via the written word, you have made a world of difference. You have not just helped me to translate ideas into a book for this purpose, but you have also taught me how to write a book. Thank you also to the phenomenal team at Greenleaf Book Group, including Justin Branch, Erin Brown, Diana Coe, Jared Dorsey, Danielle Green, Tanya Hall, Valerie Howard, Chelsea Richards, Jeanette Smith, Brian Welch, and other remarkable associates who have contributed here. You saw the potential in this book, and we have worked together to bring an offering to readers that reflects your experience, energy, and insight.

Last but not least, I want to thank my family for their continued support along the way. First, to my extraordinary wife, Mary Elizabeth—your inspiration, insight, and encouragement have meant the world to me. To Sarabeth, Louie, and Mary Adelaide, you've provided enthusiasm, ideas, and discovery all along the way. To my family more broadly, thank you for bearing with me as I expressed excitement about this idea, played with thoughts and asked questions about various related topics, and requested your support during the journey. These comments would not be complete without expressing profound gratitude to my mom and dad, who fundamentally shaped my view of the world, infused a commitment to integrity, and encouraged a wide range of experiences. To Dad, for his commitment to giving back to the community, as well as strategic thinking, customer focus, and taking care of the team. To Mom, for my multifaceted interest in lifelong learning, reading, expression, listening, and kindness combined with many conversations about the things that matter.

Simply stated, this book derives from the combined contributions of all the people here and many others. I'm eternally grateful and see this as an expression of what you've taught me and what we've experienced together.

RESOURCES

I f you want to read more about intrapreneurship, you can begin with the book that started a new wave of understanding on this topic, *Intrapreneuring* by Gifford Pinchot III. This is the book based on Pinchot's original research surrounding the concept of intrapreneurship.

Once you've got that one under your belt, branch out and read more widely about innovation. Intrapreneurs don't work in a vacuum. They are part of the larger innovation ecosystem. It makes sense for anyone interested in innovation to understand the wider landscape of the topic, not just what will go on in their corner of the marketplace.

In my interviews with intrapreneurs and innovators, I came across many recommendations for further reading. As a service to you, I offer a modest sample list of books here, while recognizing that many more offer great value and insight. I also encourage you to explore additional formats such as podcasts and other digital media. Much of what is going on in intrapreneurship can be discussed in real time on social media and other virtual platforms. It pays to stay current.

Here's a collection of books that will enhance your understanding of innovation in the marketplace today.

- *Amazon Unbound: Jeff Bezos and the Invention of a Global Empire* by Brad Stone

- *Articulating Design Decision: Communicate with Stakeholders, Keep Your Sanity, and Deliver the Best User Experience* by Tom Greever

- *Atomic Habits* by James Clear

- *Blue Ocean Strategy, Expanded Edition. How to Create Uncontested Market Space and Make the Competition Irrelevant* by W. Chan Kim and Renee A. Mauborgne

- *Business Model Generation: A Handbook for Visionaries, Game Changers, and Challengers* by Alexander Osterwalder and Yves Pigneur

- *The Business Model Navigator: 55 Models That Will Revolutionize Your Business* by Oliver Gassmann, Karolin Frankenberger, Michaela Csik

- *The Busy Leader's Handbook: How to Lead People and Places That Thrive* by Quint Studer

- *Call Me Ted* by Ted Turner with Bill Burke

- *Change by Design: How Design Thinking Transforms Organizations and Inspires Innovation* by Tim Brown

- *Competitive Strategy: Techniques for Analyzing Industries and Competitors* by Michael Porter

- *Dare to Lead* by Brené Brown

- *The Design of Business: Why Design Thinking is the Next Competitive Advantage* by Roger L. Martin

- *The Design Thinking Playbook: Mindful Digital Transformation of Teams, Products, Services, Businesses, and Ecosystems* by Michael Lewrick, Patrick Link, and Larry Leifer

- *Designing with Data: Improving the User Experience With A/B Testing* by Rochelle King

- *Designing Your Work Life: How to Thrive and Change and Find Happiness at Work* by Bill Burnett and Dave Evans

- *Discovery-Driven Growth: A Breakthrough Process to Reduce Risk and Seize Opportunity* by Rita Gunther McGrath and Ian C. Macmillan

- *The Eight Paradoxes of Great Leadership: Embracing the Conflicting Demands of Today's Workplace* by Tim Elmore

- *Essential Wisdom for Leaders of Every Generation* by Randy Hain

- *Extreme Ownership* by Jocko Willink and Leif Babin

- *The Five Dysfunctions of a Team* by Patrick Lencioni

- *The Generals* by Winston Groom

- *Good Strategy, Bad Strategy: The Difference and Why It Matters* by Richard Rumelt

- *Great by Choice* by Jim Collins

- *Grit* by Angela Duckworth
- *Hacking Growth: How Today's Fastest-Growing Companies Drive Breakout Success* by Morgan Brown and Sean Ellis
- *The Hard Thing About Hard Things* by Ben Horowitz
- *The Innovation Mindset* by Lorraine Marchand
- *The Innovator's Dilemma* by Clayton M. Christensen
- *INSPIRED: How to Create Products Customers Love* by Marty Cagan
- *Just Be Honest: Authentic Communication Strategies That Get Results and Last a Lifetime* by Steven Gaffney
- *Lead to Win* by Carla A. Harris
- *Lean Analytics: Use Data to Build a Better Startup Faster (Lean Series)* by Alistair Croll and Benjamin Yoskovitz
- *The Lean Startup* by Eric Ries
- *No Rules Rules: Netflix and the Culture of Reinvention* by Reed Hastings and Erin Meyer
- *Numbers Guide: Essentials of Business Numeracy* by The Economist
- *The Personal MBA: Master the Art of Business* by Josh Kaufman
- *Play Bigger: How Rebels and Innovators Create New Categories and Dominate Markets* by Al Ramadan, Dave Peterson, Christopher Lochhead, and Kevin Maney

- *Playing to Win: How Strategy Really Works* by Roger Martin and A. G. Lafley

- *Powershift: Transform Any Situation, Close Any Deal, and Achieve Any Outcome* by Daymond John with Daniel Poisner

- *The Slight Edge* by Jeff Olson

- *Sprint: How to Solve Big Problems and Test New Ideas in Just Five Days* by Jake Knapp, John Zeratsky, and Braden Kowitz

- *Steve Jobs* by Walter Isaacson

- *Value Proposition Design: How to Create Products and Services Customers Want* by Alexander Osterwalder, Yves Pigneur, Gregory Bernarda, Alan Smith, and Trish Papadakos

- *The Weather Channel: The Improbable Rise of a Media Phenomenon* by Frank Batten with Jeffrey L. Cruikshank

NOTES

Introduction

1. Gifford Pinchot, *Intrapreneuring* (New York: Harper & Row, 1985), ix.

Chapter 1: Start with Your Inner Game

1. Debora Wilson (former president and CEO, The Weather Channel), in discussion with the author, May 2023.

2. Derek Van Nostran (co-founder, Atlanta Interactive Marketing Association), in discussion with the author, March 2023.

3. Juan Andrés Muños (founder, Pamplonews), in discussion with the author, April 2023.

4. Quincy Johnson (vice president, operations, global media company), in discussion with the author, March 2023.

5. Doug Busk (independent consultant), in discussion with the author, April 2023.

6. Keith Wilmot (founder and managing partner, Ignitor Agency), in discussion with the author, March 2023.

7. Joe Fiveash (VP, strategy and media solutions, IBM), in discussion with the author, March 2023.

8. Aidoo Osei (senior vice president, product strategy, Global Payments), in discussion with the author, May 2023.

Chapter 2: Scan for Opportunity

1. Marie Quintero-Johnson (former vice president and head of global corporate development, The Coca-Cola Company), in discussion with the author, May 2023.

2. Tom Daly (owner, Relevant Ventures), in discussion with the author, March 2023.

3. Michael Britt (president and CEO, Southern Telecom), in discussion with the author, June 2023.

4. Jim Trupiano (director of strategy & business development, Georgia Power), in discussion with the author, June 2023.

5. Craig Kirkland (vice president, product management for mobile and multimedia, Gartner), in discussion with the author, March 2023.

6. Quint Studer (cofounder, Healthcare Plus Solutions Group), in discussion with the author, March 2023.

7. Bill Burke (founder, The Optimism Institute), in discussion with the author, May 2023.

8. Clayton M. Christensen, *The Innovator's Dilemma* (Boston: Harvard Business Review Press, 1997).

9. Joshua Sommer (new growth and development, Cox Communications), in discussion with the author, March 2023.

10. Jim DiAndreth (managing director, GP Ventures, Georgia-Pacific), in discussion with the author, May 2023.

11. Chris Walters (CEO, Avantax), in discussion with the author, May 2023.

12. Pascal Racheneur (managing director, PJR Holding), in discussion with the author, March 2023.

13. Derek Van Nostran (cofounder, Atlanta Interactive Marketing Association), in discussion with the author, March 2023.

Chapter 3: Craft the Strategy

1. Stephen Covey, *7 Habits of Highly Effective People* (New York: Simon and Schuster, 1989).

2. "About LinkedIn," LinkedIn, https://about.linkedin.com/.

3. "The IKEA Vision," IKEA, https://www.ikea.com/us/en/this-is-ikea/about-us/the-ikea-vision-and-values-pub9aa779d0.

4. Bahns Stanley (former executive vice president of strategy and development at The Weather Channel), in discussion with the author, August 2023.

5. Scot Safon (marketing strategist, Civic Entertainment Group), in discussion with the author, May 2023.

6. Decker Anstrom (former president, Landmark Communications), in discussion with the author, April 2023.

7. Eric Ries, *The Lean Startup* (New York: Crown Currency, 2011).

8. Anstrom, discussion.

9. Ashlee Adams (global director, open innovation and corporate development, The Coca-Cola Company), in discussion with the author, May 2023.

Chapter 4: Build and Sustain the Team

1. Vicki Raimey (COO of Credenza), in discussion with the author, April 2023.

2. Jim Collins, *Good to Great* (New York: HarperCollins, 2001).

3. Dr. Loretta Daniels (director of Bridge Builders at Technology Association of Georgia), in discussion with the author, March 2023.

4. Daniels, discussion.

5. WP Engine, "Generation Influence: Gen Z Study Reveals a New Digital Paradigm," WP Engine Blog, 7 July 2020, https://wpengine.com/blog/generation-influence-gen-z-study-reveals-a-new-digital-paradigm/.

6. Scot Safon (marketing strategist at Civic Entertainment Group), in discussion with the author, May 2023.

7. Raimey, discussion.

8. Daniels, discussion.

9. Paul Iaffaldano (general partner at BIP Ventures), in discussion with the author, April 2023.

10. Debora Wilson (former president and CEO of The Weather Channel), in discussion with the author, May 2023.

Chapter 5: Communicate with Care, Multidirectionally

1. Bill Burke (founder, The Optimism Institute), in discussion with the author, May 2023.

2. Rusty Friddell (EVP, Landmark Media Enterprises), in discussion with the author, May 2023.

3. Doug Busk (independent consultant), in discussion with the author, April 2023.

4. Derek Van Nostran (co-founder, Atlanta Interactive Marketing Association), in discussion with the author, March 2023.

5. Tom Daly (owner, Relevant Ventures), in discussion with the author, March 2023.

6. Joe Fiveash (VP, strategy and media solutions, IBM), in discussion with the author, March 2023.

7. Dana Miranda and Rob Watts, "What Is a RACI Chart? How This Project Management Tool Can Boost Your Productivity," Forbes Advisor, 14 December 2022, https://www.forbes.com/advisor/business/raci-chart/.

Chapter 6: Activate Your Business

1. Katie Klein (VP marketing, Comcast Business), in discussion with the author, May 2023.

2. Marty Cagan at Silicon Valley Product Group, https://www.svpg.com/.

3. Lee Scoggins (former CEO, Nextscreen), in discussion with the author, April 2023.

4. Manish Jha (chairman and CEO, Silvermine Group), in discussion with the author, May 2023.

5. Lisa West (freelance consultant), in discussion with the author, March 2023.

6. Bill Burke (founder, The Optimism Institute), in discussion with the author, May 2023.

7. Keith Wilmot (founder and managing partner, Ignitor Agency), in discussion with the author, March 2023.

8. Tom Daly (owner, Relevant Ventures), in discussion with the author, March 2023.

9. Jha, discussion.

Chapter 7: Engage the Industry

1. Pascal Racheneur (managing director, PJR Holding), in discussion with the author, March 2023.

Chapter 8: Give Back

1. Philip Nutsugah (former senior vice president, product development and management, Cox Communications), in discussion with the author, May 2023.

2. John Hancock (CEO, Junior Achievement of Georgia), in discussion with the author, May 2023.

3. "What Is 3DE?" 3DE Schools, https://www.3deschools.org/.

4. Brené Brown, *Dare to Lead* (New York: Random House, 2018).

5. Lesley Wainwright (chief legal officer, PlayOn! Sports), in discussion with the author, March 2023.

Conclusion

1. Sterling Gerdes (general manager, venture and strategy, Delta Airlines), in discussion with the author, June 2023.

2. Janet Balis (partner, marketing practice leader, EY Consulting), in discussion with the author, April 2023.

INDEX

"As a former colleague, I watched Louis lean into mobile products long before anyone could imagine the products or benefits. *The Inside Innovator* offers unique insights to empower you to create meaningful change *within* a company!"

—WONYA LUCAS, former President and CEO, Hallmark Media

"*The Inside Innovator* is full of excellent, practical advice on how to be a more effective intrapreneur, regardless of the stage of your career. Even with forty-five years in the intrapreneuring field, I still learned new ways to move ideas forward and manage setbacks. Louis Gump writes in a style that is clear, succinct, and graceful, which makes his years of experience in both intrapreneurship and entrepreneurship shine brightly to deliver lessons that are profoundly practical."

—GIFFORD PINCHOT III, coiner of the word "intrapreneur," author of *Intrapreneuring: Why You Don't Have to Leave the Corporation to Become an Entrepreneur*

PRAISE FOR
THE INSIDE INNOVATOR

"Louis Gump was one of the first people to talk to me about expanding access to information by giving people news on their mobile devices. While it is commonplace now, at the time it was transformative. He brings those same types of insights in his new book, *The Inside Innovator*. He also demystifies the term 'intrapreneurship' and makes the process accessible to people who wish to excel as leaders within larger companies. Whether you are a neuroscientist like me or in a totally different discipline, this book can help you harness your natural talents."

—**SANJAY GUPTA,** Associate Chief of Neurosurgery, Chief Medical Correspondent, #1 *New York Times* and *Wall Street Journal* best-selling author

"Drawing from my own global experience in nurturing intrapreneurial talent, Louis's book is a powerful tool for any leader seeking to drive innovation, growth, and success within their organization."

—**RALPH DE LA VEGA,** former Vice Chairman, AT&T